Under Authority

Report on Clergy Discipline

GS 1217

Under Authority

The Report
of the General Synod Working Party
reviewing Clergy Discipline
and the working
of the Ecclesiastical Courts

CHURCH HOUSE PUBLISHING
Church House, Great Smith Street, London SW1P 3NZ

Church House Publishing
Church House
Great Smith Street
London SW1P 3NZ

ISBN 0 7151 3796 4

Published 1996 for the General Synod of the Church of England by
Church House Publishing

Cover design by Sarah Hopper

Printed in England by Cromwell Press Ltd, Melksham, Wiltshire

CONTENTS

FOREWORD

We live in a society where, increasingly, morality is being privatised and the individual is all-important. All forms of authority are treated with suspicion and the exercise of discipline is unpopular.

In such a context it may come as a surprise to find the Church of England reviewing its disciplinary procedures. Nevertheless, it is both sensible and responsible for the Church to reassess from time to time whether the systems we currently have are working and to suggest changes where they do not appear to be satisfactory.

It is a review that is urgently needed. The existing procedures have not been found adequate for our situation. Even in an increasingly privatised and individualised society, the church remains essentially a *community* of believers, who are bound together as brothers and sisters in Christ. A system of discipline is essential in holding together the members.

For such an organisation the quality and accountability of its clergy are vital. They are charged with teaching, encouraging, caring and being an example of Christian living. Both the believing community and the surrounding society have this expectation. To be ordained is to be placed in a responsible office and to be available alongside all sorts of people who are in vulnerable and sensitive situations. Holy Orders only make sense as part of the whole believing community and when exercised in a responsible manner.

So we present our Report to General Synod for it to consider our recommendations for the shape of future legislation. We have sought to suggest a way forward that will allow discipline to be handled firmly, fairly, sensitively and without delay, without distracting God's people from their primary task of mission.

The Reverend Canon Alan Hawker

Chairman, The General Synod Working
Party reviewing Clergy Discipline and the
Working of the Ecclesiastical Courts

1

INTRODUCTION

Background

1.1   The Working Party has its origins, in part, in one of the recommendations (recommendation 11) contained in the Legal Aid Commission's report 'The Ecclesiastical Legal Aid System' (GS 1028), stating that a body should be established to review the law relating to the Discipline of the Clergy and the Ecclesiastical Courts. This recommendation read:

> The Ecclesiastical Jurisdiction Measure 1963 and the other legislation on clergy discipline and related matters should be reviewed by an appropriate body. . . . The review should extend to the procedures to be followed in the preliminary stages before proceedings are commenced.

1.2   The Commission's report itself sprang from widespread concern at the publicity and cost resulting from the two trials (and subsequent appeals) of the Reverend Tom Tyler who was found guilty of conduct unbecoming the office and work of a Clerk in Holy Orders. The General Synod, at the November 1992 Group of Sessions, passed the motion:

That this Synod:

> (a)   approve the recommendations summarised in the Appendix to the Report, and

> (b)   request the standing committee to ensure that action is taken to implement these recommendations, including the introduction of the necessary legislation.

1.3   The Standing Committee subsequently established the Working Party and details of our membership and meetings are contained in Appendix A.

The current legislation

1.4   The law relating to clergy discipline is mainly contained in the Ecclesiastical Jurisdiction Measure 1963 ('the 1963 Measure'). The 1963 Measure resulted from the Archbishops' Commission on the Ecclesiastical Courts, under the chairmanship of Mr Justice Lloyd-Jacob, which reported in 1954. At the time, the law relating to clergy discipline was dispersed through different Acts and Measures and many Courts existed to deal with clergy discipline cases; but many of the Courts had, in practice, fallen into disuse. The report noted, however, that under the system which then existed clergy discipline cases fell into two broad categories: those concerned with morality, unbecoming conduct, and neglect of duty; and those concerned with doctrine, ritual and ceremonial. As is well known, the 1963 Measure retained these two broad categories though within the considerably reformed framework that emerged. In respect of the first category of cases, the court of first instance was (for priests and deacons) to be the Consistory Court, the only court which remained at diocesan level. In respect of the second category, a new court, the Court of Ecclesiastical Causes Reserved, which covered the whole of the Church of England, was established.

Cases since 1963

1.5   Since the 1963 Measure came into force no disciplinary cases have been brought before the Court of Ecclesiastical Causes Reserved, although that Court has been convened twice in faculty cases. Only a few disciplinary cases have reached the stage of a trial before the Consistory Court. The cases are as follows:

The Reverend Michael Bland (1969/70) Mr Bland was an incumbent in the Diocese of Gloucester who was tried in the Consistory Court of the Diocese of Gloucester on a number of charges which could be broadly summarised as accusations of neglect of duty. Mr Bland was found guilty on all the charges and the censure was that he be deprived of his benefices. However, he successfully appealed to the Court of Arches against the decision in respect of all but one charge for which he was given a rebuke. One result of this case was a feeling that

2

the 1963 Measure was not in fact a very suitable vehicle for dealing with cases involving neglect of duty.

The Reverend Thomas Tyler (1991/2) This case, involving two trials and two appeals, concerned an allegation of adultery with two parishioners. Mr Tyler was found guilty at the first trial in the Consistory Court of the Diocese of Chichester and was deprived of his benefice and disqualified from future preferment. He appealed to the Court of Arches and the Court held that the fairness of the trial had been impugned because, as was subsequently disclosed, one of the assessors (in effect the jury) had discussed the case with Mr Tyler beforehand and formed a view. The conviction was quashed and a retrial was held at which Mr Tyler was again convicted. A second appeal to the Court of Arches was dismissed and the second conviction therefore stood. This case was pivotal in leading to the review of the Ecclesiastical Legal Aid system referred to in paragraph 1.2 and to our own review of the law relating to clergy discipline. However, it is important not to over-emphasise the relevance of this case. It was unique in involving a double trial and appeal with the consequent costs, but the subsequent tightening up of provisions relating to the Ecclesiastical Legal Aid system mean that it is unlikely that any future trial would see costs incurred on such a scale (the total cost to the Church was over £300,000). Indeed the trial of the Dean of Lincoln bears this out. However, we believe that this case has shown that a diocesan-based system of clergy discipline is not ideal in view of the strong likelihood that the accused would be known to one or more of the assessors.

The Dean of Lincoln (1995) The trial of the Dean of Lincoln (the Very Revd Brandon Jackson), which resulted in widespread publicity, was seen by many to show that the framework of the Church's disciplinary system was inappropriate to this type of case. In particular the use of procedures which were so close to those generally followed in the secular criminal jurisdiction seemed out of keeping with a case where the allegations were not criminal in their nature. A number of people also considered that it was in the interests neither of justice nor of the Church for such a case to be in the public arena. As a result many have said that there should be no repeat of this type of case which discredited the Church and its procedures.

1.6   One other circumstance, which we would wish to mention at this stage, although it was not concerned with the 1963 Measure, was the withdrawal of the licence of the **Reverend Anthony Freeman.** Mr Freeman, author of the book *God In Us,* was a Priest-in-Charge in the diocese of Chichester and diocesan continuing ministerial education officer. Following the publication of his book his licence was terminated, on notice, because his views were considered to be incompatible with his diocesan role. We have speculated as to what might have happened if Mr Freeman had been a freeholder, and we have been struck by the different levels of protection that are available to clergy who hold a freehold and to those who do not. We deal with the issues that arise from this in more detail in Chapter 5.

1.7   We can sum up some of the criticisms which have been levelled against the 1963 Measure by saying that it is perceived as being ineffective in dealing with 'non-criminal' cases, such as Mr Bland's case, where the real complaint is that of idleness, neglect of duty or unsuitability for the particular post in question, but that it does work after a fashion for those cases where it is clear that a specific act such as adultery is charged. However, it works at great cost and, in the public perception, to the discredit of the Church generally. We refer to the actual costs of these cases in Chapter 10.

1.8   There are others who would claim that the fact that so few cases have reached trial in the Consistory Court shows that the Measure works, in that it must be an effective deterrent to misconduct. We do not share this view; rather we believe that its lack of use is more connected with the inflexibility and the cost, both in monetary and publicity terms, which have been demonstrated when cases have been tried. There is much anecdotal evidence that bishops are unwilling to utilise the 1963 Measure because of the cost, both in human and financial terms. We will deal with these perceptions more fully in the next chapter.

Other factors

1.9   It is clear to us that the experience of the use to which the 1963 Measure has been put itself constitutes sufficient grounds for a review of the Church's disciplinary procedures. There are, however, other factors which need to be taken into account.

(a)   First of all disciplinary procedures in other professions or walks of life need to be examined. The nature of the ordained ministry, the existence of the clergy freehold and the fact that those in the ministry are almost exclusively dependent on the Church for the provision of housing and stipend, mean that the lives of the clergy cannot be directly compared with those in other professions. There are, however, certain similarities to the medical and legal professions and with these useful comparisons may be made. We have therefore looked widely at disciplinary procedures, but nowhere did we find a procedure which came near to that operated by the Church.

(b)   We must also take account of parishioners' expectations of their clergy. These may be said to be particularly relevant given that the laity are increasingly contributing to the cost of maintaining the ministry. We have also noted the changing attitudes of society as a whole to particular matters such as child abuse (where concern has been heightened) or in areas of sexual morality (where attitudes are more relaxed). While society's expectations should not necessarily set the standard by which clergy are judged, they are a factor to be weighed, especially as society must have confidence in clergy disciplinary arrangements.

(c)   We are also aware of the way in which society generally is more ready to resort to the law for the settling of disputes, and the repercussions that this has for the Church. This is not simply a matter of endeavouring to accommodate such an attitude but of ensuring that the procedures which we have are as flexible as they need to be to cope with these changes.

(d)   We have also taken account of disciplinary procedures in other Churches and in other Provinces of the Anglican Communion where much recent revision has made helpful reading for us.

1.10   An effective disciplinary system for the clergy is but one part of their overall terms and conditions of service. It is also important that those who, even if in a small minority of cases, wish to complain about the clergy may do so. When such a complaint is made it is to the advantage of all if the procedures to be followed are simple, clear and easily understood. These procedures should also encourage clergy who are potentially involved in disciplinary matters to seek advice and guidance, be it from friends, a trades union or legal advisers.

1.11   The other side of the coin is that alongside the discipline of the clergy we believe that the clergy need to have a system where grievances can be adequately considered and resolved. We have, accordingly, been working closely with the Steering Group on Clergy Conditions of Service on these matters. That Group has been formulating some proposals which it would wish to commend in due course, and an account of what the Group has in mind is contained in Appendix C for further reflection and debate.

1.12   In the next chapter we set out what we consider to be the disadvantages of the procedures contained in the 1963 Measure and those features which have been found to work satisfactorily.

2

THE ECCLESIASTICAL
JURISDICTION MEASURE 1963

Introduction

2.1   In this chapter we deal in more detail with what we consider to
be the advantages and disadvantages contained in the 1963 Measure's
procedures. First of all we believe it would be useful to give a brief summary of the process involved in a case under the 1963 Measure,
showing the complexities involved. For simplicity this deals only with
the process for the trial of a priest or deacon in a conduct case. The
process for the trial of a bishop follows this basic pattern with some vari-
ations. The process for a trial involving ritual etc. follows a different
course but, as we have noted in Chapter 1, this has never been used.

Proceedings under the 1963 Measure

2.2   (a)   The first action under the 1963 Measure is the laying
of a complaint charging an offence (in practice of course a great
deal will undoubtedly have already taken place before this first
formal stage is reached). A complaint may be laid by either an
authorised complainant (a person authorised by the bishop to
lay a complaint) or six or more persons on the electoral roll of
the relevant parish.

(b)   Once a complaint has been laid the bishop must afford
the accused and each complainant the opportunity of being
interviewed, individually, in private. After this the bishop must
take one of only two courses: either decide that no further steps
should be taken in the matter of the complaint, or refer the complaint for enquiry by an examiner (selected from a panel of not
less than three barristers or solicitors drawn up by a committee

appointed by the diocesan synod). There is no other option available to the bishop and 'no further action' means precisely that; there is no provision for an admonition, no matter how light.

(c)   The duty of the examiner is to enquire into the complaint for the purpose of deciding whether there is a case to answer for which the accused should be put on trial. The accused and the complainant may lay evidence before the examiner. If the examiner decides that there is a case to answer, the accused is put on trial; if not, no further action is taken.

(d)   If a trial is to take place the bishop nominates a person to promote the complaint. The chancellor of the diocese (or a sufficiently qualified person appointed by the chancellor) presides over the consistory court that hears the trial. The chancellor sits with four assessors (selected by ballot from a panel of six priests and six laymen drawn up by a committee appointed by the diocesan synod). The procedure and the rules of the court are the same as the trial of a person by a court of assize (i.e. a modern Crown Court) exercising criminal jurisdiction, and the functions of the chancellor are the same as those of a judge of that court.

(e)   If the accused is found guilty the chancellor shall decide such penalty (or censure) as is warranted. The penalties available (we deal in detail with the question of penalties in Chapter 9) are rebuke; monition; suspension; inhibition; and deprivation. If the censure to be pronounced is deprivation from the preferment held, the bishop has the power additionally to depose the cleric concerned from Holy Orders.

(f)   Appeals from judgements made in the consistory court may be made to the Court of Arches (in the Province of Canterbury) or the Chancery Court (in the Province of York). Appeals are heard by the judge of that court sitting with two clerks in Holy Orders appointed by the Prolocutor of the Province and two laymen appointed by the Chairman of the House of Laity of the General Synod.

2.3   This outline, which gives an account of those procedures which have actually been used, may not give an adequate picture of the complexities inherent in the 1963 Measure which arise from the use of different procedures for different circumstances. For example, the procedure in doctrine cases shows quite a different approach. A complaint is initially enquired into by a committee of Convocation, comprising a bishop, two priests and two chancellors, which may decide that the accused should be tried by the Court of Ecclesiastical Causes Reserved. That Court comprises two persons who hold or have held high judicial office and three persons who are or have been diocesan bishops. However, on the first conviction for the offence no censure greater than monition can be given (i.e. an order to do, or refrain from doing, a specific act). In other words an incumbent who was found guilty of preaching a great heresy could simply be told to keep quiet on the subject. A diagrammatic representation of the various processes under the 1963 Measure appears below (figure 2.1).

2.4   In addition to this outline we should also mention two other features of the 1963 Measure. The first is the power of the bishop, at any time after a complaint has been laid, with the consent of the accused, to pronounce such censure as the bishop thinks fit. The second is the power to deprive a cleric from his preferment following certain proceedings in the secular courts. These include conviction of an offence for which a sentence of imprisonment is passed and the granting of a decree of divorce in certain circumstances.

Disadvantages of this system

2.5   Amongst the disadvantages of this system which have been suggested to us, we would wish to mention the following.

(a)   The procedures are extremely complex and elaborate and because they are, fortunately, seldom invoked neither clergy in senior positions in the Church nor diocesan registrars are familiar with the whole of the present legislation.

Figure 2.1 The Ecclesiastical Jurisdiction Measure 1963 as applied to a priest or deacon

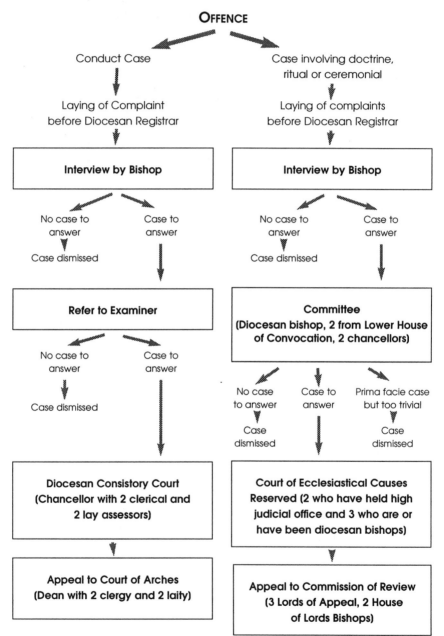

(b)   The procedures can be very expensive. In addition to any ecclesiastical legal aid granted to the accused person, the bishop, any authorised complainant, and the promoter if the case goes beyond the stage of a hearing before the examiner, will all incur legal costs, and the costs of the court and examiner will also need to be met.

(c)   There is no provision of any kind for initial mediation or conciliation, of the kind which now features in the procedure under the Incumbents (Vacation of Benefices) Measure 1977, as amended by the Incumbents (Vacation of Benefices) (Amendment) Measure 1993. Under the provisions of the 1963 Measure no disciplinary situation exists until a formal complaint is laid, by which time the opportunity for mediation will probably have passed.

(d)   There is no satisfactory 'filter' to put a stop at an early stage to cases which clearly should not be taken any further. The 1963 Measure entrusts the first stage of this function to the diocesan bishop, but even with the advice of his diocesan registrar he is often not in the best position to discharge it, and the Measure gives him no clear guidance on the criteria he is to apply. In some cases he may be too close to the complaint, because he himself may have initiated it, or it may have originated with one of his suffragan bishops or archdeacons after discussion with him. Conversely, it is very difficult for the diocesan bishop to refuse to allow a complaint of, for example, serious sexual misconduct to proceed, even if he believes that the allegations are untrue and result from psychological problems or ulterior motives.

(e)   By the time the case reaches the stage of a hearing before an examiner, considerable expense will have been incurred and the problems mentioned in (i) below will have arisen. Moreover, the examiner has no power to stop a case going forward to trial on any grounds other than that there is no case to answer; for example, if there is a case to answer on some of the allegations, the examiner cannot halt the proceedings on the grounds that although those allegations, taken alone, would amount to an ecclesiastical offence they are trivial and should be dealt with pastorally.

(f)   It is not satisfactory for the facts of the case to be tried and determined by a court which includes clergy and lay people drawn from the diocese itself. By the time the case reaches this stage, it will normally be very difficult or impossible to find suitable people within the diocese to serve on the court who do not know or have some knowledge of the accused person and who have not heard about and discussed the case itself. Similar problems can arise about providing for the case to be heard by an examiner or judge closely associated with the diocese, although the chancellor can of course ask for another judge to hear the case.

(g)   Some examiners and chancellors have more experience of court procedures of a quasi-criminal nature than others and some chancellors have their main expertise in other areas. This, coupled with the infrequency with which cases are tried, means that the level of expertise required is not available on a consistent basis between dioceses. It could also be a disadvantage that, because the chancellor might be required to hear a case, he would be unable to offer advice at the earlier stages.

(h)   It is questionable whether the treatment of the Church's disciplinary procedures as criminal or quasi-criminal is necessary or helpful, although we believe it is right to retain in such cases the use of the same burden of proof and rules of evidence as are applicable in criminal cases.

(i)   Once proceedings under the 1963 Measure get beyond the initial stages, they frequently give rise to much unfavourable publicity, which is harmful to the Church and also to an accused person who is eventually acquitted.

(j)   Because of the cost and complexity of the present system, some cases where serious misconduct has clearly occurred and where it would be appropriate for disciplinary proceedings to be taken are merely dealt with by accepting the resignation of the person concerned and having his name entered on the Archbishops' Caution List. We have more to say about the Caution List in Chapter 5.

Positive features of the 1963 Measure

2.6   The procedure and conduct of trials under the 1963 Measure are, we believe, scrupulously fair to the accused, and this is a major point in favour of those procedures. However, other than this fundamental point, the positive features of the present system which have been suggested to us lie outside the trial procedures. In fact these features will be amongst the most frequently used provisions of the 1963 Measure. We would mention the following:

(a)   The power to pronounce censure by consent (section 31 of the 1963 Measure) is one which has been found to be useful in many cases and we believe that its existence helps to mitigate the tendency to deal with cases in the way mentioned in paragraph 2.5 (j). However, in order to proceed under this section a formal complaint must first be laid. Where this has not happened some cases, which might suitably have been dealt with in accordance with these provisions, are perhaps dealt with simply by accepting a resignation. Similarly we believe that a number of cases which are commenced under these provisions are in fact resolved by the cleric's resignation and the inclusion of the cleric's name in the Archbishops' Caution List (see Chapter 5). In both cases this is unsatisfactory because, as no censure is pronounced, no formal finding of guilt is recorded. However, where the provisions of section 31 are properly used, not only does it provide a satisfactory way of dealing with clergy who accept their wrongdoing without the need for an expensive and elaborate trial, but it also opens up the possibility of mediation with an outcome satisfactory to all the parties. We are, however, conscious that this procedure takes no account of the views of the complainant, who might be dissatisfied with the eventual outcome. Moreover, the procedure, which is one between the bishop and the accused, can result in differences, both of practice and in the type of censure pronounced, from one bishop to another, and this inconsistency can itself create a sense of injustice.

(b)   The provisions for deprivation following proceedings in secular courts (section 55 of the 1963 Measure) have also been found to be helpful, although we understand that the secular courts do not always properly inform the ecclesiastical authorities of convictions or findings of a matrimonial court, and some erring clerics may have escaped notice. These provisions will, in any event, need reconsideration because of the divorce reforms contained in the Family Law Act, but the basic premise is sound.

(c)   The provisions for inhibition *pendente lite* (section 77 of the 1963 Measure) whereby an accused cleric can be inhibited from performing any services pending the outcome of the proceedings once a complaint has been lodged – which could be some time after the allegations initially come to light – are also useful. However, the circumstances under which this power is available could be said to be insufficient in that the bishop can only inhibit the cleric concerned at a time when the proceedings are pending, and he may prevent the cleric only from taking services. There might be circumstances which could warrant inhibition at an earlier stage, for example where the allegations are serious and immediate total inhibition may be the right way forward. We are conscious that this might be seen as the wrong response where allegations are later found to be maliciously conceived. Nevertheless this type of provision could be seen as safeguarding the position of all parties.

Scope of review

2.7   It seemed to us that, in view of these criticisms and the actual experience of the workings of the Measure as outlined in Chapter 1, a review of the whole of the Church's disciplinary procedures was necessary and that nothing would be gained by starting from the premise that the current system was basically sound but in need of some improvements.

2.8   In order to inform our review we sought information about disciplinary procedures from those professions which we considered to have a similar ethos to that of the Church. We also sought information from other Churches both within the Anglican Communion and outside it. We also invited submissions from members of the General

Synod and from other interested parties by giving notification of our activities in the Church Press. A list of the submissions which we received and considered (apart from a few submitted on a confidential basis) is set out in Appendix B.

2.9   It seemed clear to us that our review of this legislation first needed to be properly grounded in certain basic principles, which we set out in the next chapter.

3

BASIC PRINCIPLES

3.1   In the Church of England all who are admitted to Holy Orders have to make the Declaration of Assent. This they do at their Ordination, and on each subsequent occasion when they begin a new appointment. In so doing they affirm a commitment to the Holy Scriptures and to the Church of England's historic formularies. So it is to these sources that, in the first instance, we turn for guidance.

The Scriptures

3.2   That God is a God of justice and mercy is as basic to the theology of the New Testament as to the Old Testament. In the Parable of the Prodigal Son (Luke 15. 11-32) Christ himself draws upon the teaching of both Hosea and Amos. For the father in the parable not only *forgives* the prodigal but exercises absolute fairness towards his other son. '*All that I have is yours*' – the inheritance was not redivided. In the Epistles, these two aspects of God's character are carefully balanced. St Paul, for example, in the Epistle to the Romans, in his interpretation of the atonement, demonstrates how both the justice and mercy of God were in action. It is the crucified Christ who calls us to follow him. Our response to his gracious initiative on our behalf is joyful obedience, for '*You are not your own; you were bought at a price*' (1 Corinthians 6.20). In Christ, we are a new creation, with new values, new perspectives, and new norms of behaviour (cf. 2 Corinthians 5.16f, Colossians 3.1f, Ephesians 2.10, 1 Peter 2. 9-12, et al.). To follow Jesus is not easy, nor is it without cost. It involves entering into a teacher/pupil relationship, described in the Gospels and Acts of the Apostles as 'discipleship'.

3.3   This calling is to all believers, without exception. We are all called into a new community where old style divisions are irrelevant

(Galatians 3. 26-29, Ephesians 2.14). Together, we seek to understand the way of Christ, and to apply it in daily life (Colossians 2 6-7).

3.4   The New Testament is evidence of the desire of the early church to grapple with the implications of the new life in Christ - clarifying belief, determining appropriate behaviour, facing up to specific problems. Not least among the specific problems that arose was how to cope with failure among the believers, and wilful deviation from the commonly held norm of understanding within the community.

3.5   What is incontestable from the New Testament material is the primacy of the *agape* (love) principle. Followers of Jesus are called to love one another as Jesus loves them (John 13. 34-35, 1 John 3.11, 16; 4. 16-21). This they seek to do as they live by the grace of God and the empowering of the Holy Spirit, in conformity to the teaching and the earthly example of Jesus.

3.6   Consequently, disharmony within the community was bound to be a serious matter. Euodia and Syntyche are urged to agree with each other (Philippians 4. 2-3). But there is also realism in the urge to agree: *'If it is possible, as far as it depends on you, live at peace with everyone'* (Romans 12.18). Where there is disharmony the desired solution is reconciliation. There was a need to work towards a mutually acceptable resolution of the disagreement or dispute. This remains the preferred manner for handling disharmony and disputes to the present day.

3.7   Wherever possible the Scriptures look towards a private reconciliation. If this proves to be unattainable, then individual fellow believers should try to assist. Failing this, the wider community should become involved. And only if the brother or sister in dispute resists the guidance of the community should expulsion, regretfully, be considered (Matthew 18. 15-17, 1 Corinthians 5. 1-5).

3.8   Throughout, the understanding is that discipline will be 'in-house'. Recourse to the secular courts for settling disputes and for exercising discipline amongst believers is seen as unnecessary and inappropriate. These are internal matters for the believing community (1 Corinthians 6. 1-6). Ideally, fellow Christians should learn to forgive each other, as Christ forgave them (Colossians 3.13).

3.9   But, inevitably and sadly, because of sinfulness, occasions will arise when reconciliation is not achieved. Then it becomes necessary for the dispute to be adjudicated. *'Tell it to the church'* (Matthew 18.17), and the threat of an apostolic intervention to resolve the matter (1 Corinthians 5. 1-5) are the beginnings of a disciplinary procedure within the church. Sometimes conflicting allegations need to be heard, weighed, and assessed. At other times, a proven but unrepentant wrongdoer needs to be reprimanded.

3.10   Discipline is already being exercised in the primitive church of the New Testament. It stands as a witness to, and an emphasis of, several truths that were held to be important.

● There were boundaries to the limits of acceptable belief. Even though in the Acts of the Apostles there can be a wrestling with what is acceptable (e.g. chapters 10-11, 15), as we progress through the Epistles, the warnings to beware of false teachers grow.

● The conduct that is consistent with a Christian profession of belief is also gradually refined. Classic passages like the one on holy living in Colossians 3, with its *'putting to death'* and its *'clothing yourselves'* map out the limits of acceptable behaviour.

● The responsibility of the individual is emphasised. We are stewards who will be held personally accountable. So we need to stand answerable for our belief and our behaviour.

● Important though the individual is, the community matters as well. So there is within the burgeoning discipline of the early church a desire to protect the believing community and its mission.

● Discipline was exercised in the hope that it would encourage repentance; a 'coming to their senses' and a 'putting right' of that which was wrong. So, even in the most serious cases, there was always the longing for a fresh commitment to the way of Christ, and the hope that it might be possible to move on from the past.

The Scriptures and clergy discipline

3.11   Those called to leadership in Holy Orders are part of the 'laos' of God. The general expectations of discipleship are as applicable to them as they are to any believer. Yet, from Old Testament times onward, they come to be treated differently, and more stringently, than the rest of God's people. In Leviticus 21.8 the people are instructed to '*regard them as holy*', and it becomes a consistent theme that more is expected of their religious leaders. The judgement on Eli's two sons, and the appointment of Samuel, revolves around God's desire to '*raise up a faithful priest, who will do according to what is in my heart and mind*' (1 Samuel 2.35). Ezekiel warns against unfaithful shepherds of God's people, and God says, '*I will hold them accountable for my flock*' (Ezekiel 34.10). The prophet also takes up the 'watchman' theme (in Ezekiel 3.16f and 33.1f), and God '*will hold the watchman accountable*' (a theme that reappears in Hebrews 13.17). Micah 3 and Malachi 2: 1-9 go on to highlight the particular answerability of leaders and priests.

3.12   In the New Testament this emphasis on separate and more rigorous treatment is continued. Clergy are to '*set an example*' (1 Timothy 4.12, Titus 2.7). Believers are urged to '*Remember your leaders, who spoke the word of God to you. Consider the outcome of their way of life and imitate their faith*' (Hebrews 13.7). So those who presume to teach '*will be judged more strictly*' (James 3:1). Not least, this is because they are expected to have some maturity in the faith (1 Timothy 3.6). But, to balance this, because of their more public and noticeable position, which makes them especially vulnerable to attack, particular care is to be taken in protecting them from unwarranted allegations and slurs (1 Timothy 5.19).

3.13   What is surprising in 1 Timothy 3 are the qualities being sought. Clergy are not required to exemplify an advanced and higher standard. Rather, they are called to demonstrate qualities that we would delight to find in every believer. But whilst these are the norm towards which the whole church aspires, in the clergy there is to be a reliable and consistent delivery. This can only be, of course, by the grace of God and in the power of the Holy Spirit. But he who calls is also well able to equip.

The Christian tradition

3.14   The nascent disciplinary structure of the New Testament continued to develop down the centuries. Before AD 310 it concentrated mainly on internal church life. After Constantine's conversion, it expanded to cover a far wider area of jurisdiction. Marriage and family relationships came under ecclesiastical jurisdiction, and other areas too. At times this wider responsibility grew, and at other times it was restricted.

3.15   Alongside the developing discipline of the church came a growing organisational structure. It was not long before the bishop was assisted by officers and by a court. Both adjudication and the enforcement of decisions developed.

3.16   The distinguishing of clergy as a distinct group disciplined in a particular way also developed. In the early sixth century, for instance, Finnian of Clonard, in one of the earliest methodical penitentiaries, distinguishes quite sharply between the fairly mild penances that the laity can be given, and the more demanding exercises considered appropriate for the clergy.

3.17   It is this continuing and refining response to discipline down the centuries that is the basis of the church's Canon Law. *'The canons are norms and standards of Christian behaviour . . . They have but one purpose – to keep the church from evil and to prescribe what is necessary or useful to the living of life'* (R.C. Mortimer, *Western Canon Law*).

3.18   **'The Canons of the Church of England'** trace their history back down the centuries, through the developing Canon Law of Western Christendom. Our present Canons continue to reflect the same disciplinary concerns.

- They repeatedly emphasise the importance of *'virtuous conversation and good repute'* (C 4.1, 8.2a, 10.2, 12.2). *'Former good life and behaviour'* is an alternative phrase to make this point.

- Alongside good living there is placed the requirement to be *'a wholesome example'* to the flock of Christ (C 4.1, C18).

- Canon C 26 goes on to suggest that those in Holy Orders need to be single-minded in following their calling. To this end some *'occupations, habits, or recreations'* are inimical to this calling. Equally, this Canon highlights the point that there are duties entailed in Holy Orders, which the Minister is expected to fulfil in all normal circumstances.

- A Minister can be refused appointment (C 10.3) on various grounds. These include *'grave misconduct or neglect of duty in an ecclesiastical office, evil life, having by his conduct caused grave scandal concerning his moral character since his ordination'*.

- Bishops are required to exercise discipline within their diocese (C 18.7), and those in Holy Orders can be deprived or deposed, i.e. disciplined, by *'legal and canonical process'* within the Church of England.

The historic formularies of the Church of England

3.19   The Thirty-nine Articles of Religion make little reference to the discipline of the clergy.

- Article 26 recognises that *'the evil be ever mixed with the good'*. Where evil Ministers exist, enquiry should occur, charges be brought, and the offender *'finally being found guilty, by just judgement be deposed'*.

- Article 34, whilst not requiring ceremonial to be totally uniform, does nevertheless expect some measure of consistency across the Church of England. Ministers 'doing their own thing' is deplored, and such clergy should *'be rebuked openly'*.

3.20   The Ordinal, as we might expect, relates much more closely to discipline. In both The Book of Common Prayer and in *The Alternative Service Book*, 1980, the Ordination Services provided for Deacons, Priests and Bishops indicate very clearly the expectations and standards that the church requires of those who are in Holy Orders. These standards are to be found throughout, in the Prefaces, the Bible readings, the Collects, and the Examinations.

21

(a)   They are to be men and women with a good reputation.

(b)   They are to be of *'godly life and sound learning'*. This regularly used couplet emphasises both behaviour and Christian understanding. Not only is this to be true at Ordination, but the candidates are asked to make a commitment to continue in this manner, framing and fashioning their lives so that they are *'adorned with innocency of life'*.

(c)   The reason for such high standards is *'the treasure now to be entrusted to you'*, i.e. God's people. So important are their needs that only the best possible leadership is acceptable for them. So the clergy are to be *'wholesome and godly examples and patterns for the people to follow'*. This is why the BCP speaks of the *'dignity and importance of the Office'*, and of the *'weighty'* responsibility of Holy Orders.

(d)   For Bishops at their Consecration the same emphases are repeated. But to them is added the responsibility to uphold the discipline of the church, both as guardian of truth, and as judge of misbehaviour – *'and such as be unquiet, disobedient and criminous, within your Diocese, correct and punish'*. In doing so the bishop is to *'so minister discipline that [he] forget not mercy'*. And this is all towards the edifying and making perfect of Christ's people.

3.21   So it is clear from Scripture, from the pages of Christian history, and in the historic formularies of the Church of England that those in Holy Orders are required to be a disciplined group of leaders, open to discipline if and when they fall short of the standards that they exemplify and by which they live.

3.22   But clergy are not 'superhuman'. They are, as is true of all God's people, both human and sinful, reliant upon the grace and love of God in Christ. They are, in the words of 2 Corinthians 4 (ASB Ordination of a Bishop, Epistle), *'no better than pots of earthenware to contain this treasure'*. Consequently, as the Priest candidate is informed, they *'cannot bear the weight of this ministry in [their] own strength'*. So, whilst we must be prepared to discipline our clergy, the entire church needs also to pray constantly for them in their grave responsibilities. As the bishop prays in the Ordinal, we too must pray that our clergy may be given the will to serve faithfully, and may also be granted the divine strength and power to do so.

A distinctive ministry and answerability

3.23   It may be that some would wish to disagree with the idea of the clergy being treated differently from, and more rigorously than, the rest of the believing community. But not only is this found in the Scriptures and the Christian tradition, it also accords with secular and rational judgement.

3.24   In the representations we received, and the enquiries that we made, it was noticeable that no one challenged this premise:

- the various professions all acknowledge that their practitioners are to be assessed distinctively in the light of their professional position;

- other church denominations clearly distinguish between those in positions of leadership, and the remainder of the membership;

- the secular courts treat misdemeanours by persons in positions of trust much more seriously than similar offences by others.

3.25   We speak of those in Holy Orders being set apart for the office and work of ministry. This is both a responsibility and a privilege. Ordinary church members look to their clergy and trust them. Within the Church, those in Holy Orders accept:

- **an institutional responsibility** – to them is allocated the per-formance of roles considered to be central and essential to the Church's life;

- **a teaching responsibility** – they are trained to be able to feed the flock, clarifying and explaining Scripture, belief and behav-iour;

- **a representative responsibility** – for many in our society they stand for the Church, and are seen to speak on its behalf;

● **a responsibility to be an example** – 'practise what you preach' is a fair demand. Clergy are expected to live a sacrificial life of self-denial in such a way that both the Church and society are provided with a wholesome and attractive demonstration of godly living;

● **a responsibility of confidentiality** – clergy become involved in situations of confidentiality, or where people are particularly vulnerable. These occur both within the Church and in society generally, and demand a more than usually careful standard of responsibility.

3.26   It is, therefore, not unreasonable that the Church should determine the standards to be expected of its clergy. This is essential for the protection of the Church and those it seeks to serve. It is vital if the Church's leadership is to serve with the confidence of the laity. It is necessary for the clergy, so that they know clearly what is expected of them. And this discipline will cover several areas:

● the performance of their allocated duties;

● their adherence to the Faith as the Church understands it;

● their style of life and conduct;

● their maintenance of the highest professional standards in the situations of vulnerability in which they often serve.

3.27   To fall short in any or each of these areas constitutes an 'ecclesiastical offence'. The Church has to take such failures seriously. As we are all forgiven and forgiving sinners, repentance and reconciliation will be a principal concern. But even when this is possible, the viability of the cleric's being permitted to continue in office, conditionally or at all, will still have to be addressed. Sometimes immediate restoration will be appropriate; in other cases, only after an interval of time has passed; sometimes, and very sadly, not at all. For whilst all may continue to serve Christ beyond repented sin, Holy Orders may not be a realistic avenue for some to continue in their service of Christ.

3.28   Alongside the protection afforded to the Church and to Holy Orders, we need also to be concerned with protecting our clergy. Many are making the sacrifices of limited remuneration and living in housing not their own. So allegations of an offence can create a serious crisis for them. Not only is their source of income imperilled, but also their home. Consequently, the Church has an obligation to protect its clergy from frivolous, spiteful and maliciously motivated accusations. Especially this is so because clergy are particularly vulnerable to rumour and slur. So it is vital that the disciplinary procedures should be meticulous in providing protection and dealing robustly with the malicious and the mischievous on behalf of their clergy, but not to the extent of failing to search out and fairly determine guilt when it exists. The innocent must feel secure, and investigations, when necessary, must be handled sensitively, fairly, and promptly. To fall short in these objectives would render any system of discipline weak, uncertain, and ineffective.

3.29   Enshrined within the procedures there will need to be the best practice available. As part of our society, the Church must co-operate with the secular authorities wholeheartedly. There is no place for cover-ups where the law of the land or the concerns of our society are relevant. Nor, when exercising its own internal discipline, would it ever be acceptable for the Church to offer its clergy procedures of discipline that were less generous or less fair than those which they could reasonably expect in a secular court of law. Ecclesiastical practice should be a model of best practice, interlaced with a desire to seek reconciliation where this is possible. Those accused of an ecclesiastical offence should be expected to be treated firmly and fairly, yet with graciousness and mercy.

3.30   We found particular assistance to this end in a review of what are often termed '**the rules of natural justice**'. These basic rules, to which our modern Western democracies adhere, originate in part from the development of a Christian understanding of justice. Some of these rules were formulated in the courts of the medieval church. So they are consistent with a Christian approach. Indeed, the Church should rejoice at their wide acceptance today, and adhere to them in its own disciplinary procedures.

Basic principles of natural justice

3.31   The ruling principle is that of *transparency*. Procedures need to be open and observable. For not only must justice be achieved; it should be clearly and openly seen to be done.

3.32   The person against whom allegations are made must always be told in full what they are, and normally (unless there is very good reason to withhold it) he should be told the identity of his accusers.

3.33   The accused person must always be allowed to defend himself. So this will mean:

● the accused should be given time to prepare a defence - no pressure for immediate responses

● the accused should always be allowed to be heard in his own defence, and be given the opportunity to cross-examine those who have accused him

● the accused should be allowed an accompanying friend or representative if he so wishes, so that he does not have to stand trial alone, unless he prefers to do so

● no one should (saving extremely exceptional circumstances) be tried in his absence.

3.34   No one shall be judge in his own case. We need to avoid both conflict of interest and vested interest. So:

● no one shall be allowed to be judge as well as accuser, witness or jury, or in any way discharge more than one of these functions

● no one who can be shown to be acting out of malice or to be prejudiced against the accused should be allowed to be accuser, judge, jury, or witness.

The chief practical issue here is discussed more fully in Chapter 4 (paragraphs 5 and 6). So the need for ground rules is essential.

3.35   There must always be a right of appeal. This should be to an impartial and higher authority, with powers to enforce any decisions reached on appeal. And as dissatisfaction can be in the *manner* of handling the procedures rather than in the technical content, there is a case for some sort of grievance procedure as well. Reference to this is made in Chapter 5 (paragraphs 37 to 39).

3.36   Justice delayed unduly is also justice denied. The procedure needs to be capable of providing a fair and expeditious investigation of complaints. So we are suggesting that there should be clear time-scales within which, normally, proceedings should be completed.

3.37   Whilst we do not wish to generate complaints, we do believe that those who feel aggrieved should be able to express their complaint. In the first instance they should not need to set out their allegation in legal or technical terms, though it should always be in writing.

3.38   A complaint having been made, the burden of proof should lie with the complainant. It is the responsibility of the person making the complaint to substantiate it, not of the accused cleric to disprove it. Furthermore, the present burden of proof required is '*beyond all reasonable doubt*', and we see no reason to alter or to reduce that burden of proof.

3.39   Given the acceptability of these principles, it is vital that they be adhered to by all. It must come to be understood that 'short cuts', to save time, for instance, or because the evidence is deemed to be overwhelming – cannot and will not be tolerated. Indeed, failure to adhere to the procedures, or an individual's 'doing their own thing', might very well come to be a disciplinary offence in its own right.

3.40   To assist in meeting these criteria, we propose that there should be, in addition to the disciplinary procedure, some 'Codes of Practice'. These would be to advise and guide the bishop and his advisers. The problem with legislation is that it takes considerable time to enact, and so in a Measure we want to provide a relevant simplified procedure for discipline, with sufficient flexibility to have enduring value. Alongside the Measure (but required by it) there will be guidance to highlight best practice, and to define appropriate ways of carrying through the procedure. In the light of experience, such practices will need to be modified. Using a Measure would be a lengthy and tortuous route. In Codes of Practice laid before the General Synod for approval modifications can be made effectively and swiftly, without undue fuss, but in a responsible and accountable way.

3.41   The function of Codes of Practice, which should remain short and simple rather than become complex and confusing, is not to dictate style. They are there to warn against 'short cuts' in handling discipline, and to ensure a fair hearing. So often nowadays in law the substance of the issue is not addressed because the case is argued over technicalities and neglect of proper practice. Codes should guard against this and enable the substance of the complaint to be assessed and responded to. So Codes of Practice provide a framework of security for everyone concerned. The bishop or his agent is perceived to have investigated fairly, and not to be placing undue pressure on complainant or cleric. The cleric involved is assured of his right to defend himself with help. Precipitate action is avoided and ongoing grievances should only surround the decision reached, not the procedure by which it was reached. These Codes of Practice will be advisory, not mandatory, but they will reflect best practice in handling disciplinary issues.

Some of the practical consequences

3.42   As indicated at the end of Chapter 2, we deemed it wise to 'go back to the drawing board' and rebuild the Church's disciplinary procedure. At the core of our proposals is a body called a tribunal rather than a court. The European Court has ruled that courts are tribunals, and tribunals are courts. We agree, and wish to stress that in no way will due legal process be lost or compromised by our suggested way forward. Adjudications will continue to be chaired by persons with significant legal qualification and experience who will be responsible to ensure due process. But a tribunal means:

- a wide range of people with relevant skills will be involved;

- a more flexible approach will be possible;

- hearings should be more cost-effective than at present;

- whilst adjudications will remain public, hearings do not have to be so unless this is felt to be advantageous in the particular case;

- the change of terminology will be psychologically helpful, ensuring that the new procedures are not tainted by the dislikes and criticisms (be these fair or unfair) attaching to the present system.

Yet to have a tribunal and greater flexibility does not mean a loss of due process or any of the essentials of a fair trial.

3.43   Both senior and junior clergy will need to be acquainted with the rules.   To be ignorant of the procedures, or, knowing them, yet still to 'bend' them or to ignore them, cannot be treated lightly.

3.44   The new system we propose will require some in-service training for those who have to operate it. There will need to be a more systematic and rigorous written record of telephone conversations, interviews and other contacts. Alertness to the reasons for the required procedures (however irksome they may at times feel) will be essential.

3.45   We consider it vital that the Church should have confidence that something will be done on those occasions, albeit we hope rarely, when things go wrong. Failure of good practice needs to be as open to investigation as are complaints. Where injustices occur they must be corrected, and an apology made by the person in authority who is at fault (see Chapter 5, paragraphs 37 to 39).

4

THE ROLE OF THE BISHOP

4.1   Throughout Christian history the bishop (or his leadership equivalent) has been involved in discipline. This is seen as an integral part of his oversight. That discipline relates to the entire Christian community. But increasingly and specifically, the bishop has had a direct concern for the discipline of the clergy. For it is the bishop who ordains, who appoints and licenses. The clergy are seen as sharing in ministry with the bishop. So it is he who, logically, should also suspend a delinquent pastor.

4.2   The Ordinal (both in the BCP and ASB) places a firm emphasis upon the bishop's disciplinary responsibility. As we saw in Chapter 3 (paragraph 20 (d)) he is urged to '*minister discipline*' as part of his overall obligation to be a guardian of the faith.

4.3   To this day the bishop is the Ordinary, the church official having ecclesiastical jurisdiction over his territory. His ordinary jurisdiction requires him to exercise discipline, as well as pastoral care, teaching, and a sacramental ministry.

4.4   We propose that this central involvement of the bishop in the area of clergy discipline should be reaffirmed. Not only should it be retained, but the structures for discipline should be so designed as to allow the bishop to be involved earlier in the process, and with a greater measure of flexibility.

4.5   However, we need to bear in mind that discipline is not the bishop's only, or primary, responsibility. As leader of the eucharistic community he has, by implication, a ministry of reconciliation. He is also called, as the Shepherd, to care for and to pastor the flock. This will include affirming and encouraging clergy, amongst others. And this is particularly vital for those who are struggling to meet the demands of their vocation. Often he will be the confidant of his clergy, and party to sensitive and highly personal information.

4.6   There will be occasions when it will be very difficult for the bishop to be both a pastor, and also the one administering discipline. There is bound at times to be role-conflict. The furtherance of either role can be, and often is, detrimental to the satisfactory execution of the other. This places the bishop in a potentially impossible position. Similar role-conflicts occur in other areas (the teacher in the classroom), so this is not uniquely a problem for bishops. But we do expect neutrality and transparency when someone is called upon to adjudicate. So the bishop will be under pressure to opt for one responsibility at the expense of the other, or he may rashly attempt at times to act in both roles and to disregard the conflict between them.

4.7   It is useful, therefore, to remember that, in all his responsibilities, the bishop ministers as a servant of the believing community. The early New Testament references (Matthew 18. 15-20, 1 Corinthians 5. 1-5) emphasise this communal context. Consequently the Church has never understood the bishop as acting entirely on his own. Structures have been developed to help him, and officers provided to assist him in ensuring that discipline is satisfactorily handled. For many years the Consistory Court and its officials have stood evidence to this communal involvement with and alongside the bishop in the exercise of his disciplinary authority.

4.8   We are proposing that the bishop should continue to be assisted in the exercise of discipline. But we are proposing a new structure (set out in detail in Chapter 7) which we suggest will be better suited to give him that assistance.

4.9   Detailed awareness of legal procedure, and an alertness to the subtle nuances so critical in a judicial enquiry, are not, and should not be, prerequisites for appointment to episcopal office. Nor should a bishop be expected to be proficient in understanding what is, or what is not, admissible in the evidence supporting a complaint or allegation. Neither is a bishop necessarily well placed to review evidence and determine whether a prima facie case exists. All this advice and support is already made available to a bishop. It should continue to be made available, and bishops should be encouraged to make proper use of this assistance.

31

4.10   An analogy can be drawn with the bishop's responsibility to ordain. Whilst the decision is, quite clearly, the bishop's, he is provided with a range of resources to advise him. Both in the initial selection of the candidates, and in their ongoing preparatory training, the bishop rightly relies substantially on these resources to inform and advise him.

4.11   In a similar way, we are proposing that resources appropriate to our present needs be provided to assist the bishop in carrying through his disciplinary responsibilities. Until now this has been part of the function of the bishop's own Consistory Court. But for reasons outlined in Chapter 2, we no longer see this as adequate. Not least this is because of the very local nature of the Consistory Court. We believe it would be better for future discipline to have a national or provincial context.

4.12   The new arrangements that we are proposing will, we believe:

- provide a greater degree of flexibility;
- allow for greater consistency across the dioceses;
- be more 'user-friendly' for everyone involved;
- make the procedures easier for all parties to understand.

But, unlike our analogy with ordination selection, in the more serious and/or contested cases of discipline, a neutral panel will carry through adjudication and censure on behalf of the bishop.

4.13   Alongside the proposed disciplinary procedure, we are equally concerned to provide a means of offering advice to the bishops, highlighting the best practice, advising on appropriate censures, and encouraging consistency across the Church.

4.14   Bishops vary widely in their personal evaluation of what constitutes an ecclesiastical offence, how seriously an offence should be treated, and to what extent mitigating circumstances should be considered. Representations made to us indicate that in some areas, one bishop will expect resignation whilst another takes no action at all, over a similar offence! Where this happens, a sense of injustice is unavoidable, especially where the response can only be explained in terms of the incidence of personality and geography. That each bishop will vary in outlook and response is neither unexpected nor to be deplored. But some measure of reasonable consistency is to be expected, and this cannot be guaranteed at a diocesan level. Failure to be consistent will also suggest a church unable to identify common standards, and open to the charge of being arbitrary in its exercise of discipline.

4.15   We would also wish to emphasise the need to protect God's people. All too easily discipline can become individualised. Neither the needs of the allegedly erring cleric, nor the personal standpoint of the particular bishop, are the whole of the story. It is the need of the believing community for high-quality and reliable leadership that is paramount. The individual bishop's personal exercise of *episcope* does matter. The needs of the cleric in trouble must be handled fairly, promptly, and, if at all possible, compassionately. But none of these concerns must be allowed to override the paramount concern of God's people for proper protection, and grounds for confidence in their leaders.

5

SPECIFIC ISSUES
THAT NEED TO BE FACED

5.1   It was the Lloyd-Jacob Report of 1954, in recommending a drastic reduction in the 'jungle of courts' then in existence, that led directly to the Ecclesiastical Jurisdiction Measure of 1963. It was a major step forward, though it was very much a child of its time. Chapter 2 has already highlighted the growing dissatisfaction felt over the 1963 Measure, which has led to this review. Early in our review it became apparent that the 1963 Measure was not appropriate for minor modification. We came to the conclusion that it would be necessary to start afresh, with a clean sheet of paper.

5.2   We are persuaded that the time has come to introduce a new and essentially simpler system. We are, therefore, proposing one procedure, to be common to all types of disciplinary cases. It will cover cases involving doctrine, ritual and ceremonial. The result of this will be that, in discipline cases, there will be no further need for the Court of Ecclesiastical Causes Reserved (though it will remain for faculty cases). The same simplified procedure will also handle cases of discipline involving bishops.

5.3   Alongside this proposed unitary procedure is the need to ensure the independence of the adjudication procedure. To this end we propose that the new tribunal system should be organised nationally. To achieve this we also propose to leave most of Part 1 of the 1963 Measure in place (thus preserving the diocesan-based Consistory Courts and their Faculty Jurisdiction), but remove from the Consistory Courts their disciplinary role.

5.4   We believe that the new procedures will be more flexible, and easier to operate. We envisage that alongside the statutory provisions, there will be some Codes of Practice. For instance, if in the middle of a pastoral interview with one of his clergy a bishop realises that an issue of discipline is involved, how should he proceed? A Code of Practice will indicate how to act so as not to override the principles of natural justice outlined in Chapter 3.

5.5   Whilst we are confident that the legislative core structure will be relevant and usable for a long time to come, the Codes of Practice will be more readily open to modification and refinement in the light of experience. In this way the new procedure for discipline will encourage a built-in critique, that keeps practice abreast of the latest thinking, without endless recourse to legislation.

The Caution List

5.6   Ever since 1908 a list of clergy who are under discipline has been in existence. For a long time this was a virtually unknown fact. More recently it has become more widely known, although a lot of ignorance remains about it. This directory is known as The Archbishops' Caution List, although it may soon be given the new title of The Lambeth and Bishopthorpe Register.

5.7   The List is updated every three months, and a copy is circulated to each diocesan and area bishop. It is not available to suffragan bishops, nor archdeacons, and the List has not been seen by members of the Working Party. So its content of names is truly confidential. However, the Working Party has been fully briefed on the nature of the List and on its current procedures. We wish to record our appreciation to those involved for the time they have given us, and for their openness to be questioned by us.

5.8   The List falls into two main parts. The first part is a record of those on whom a censure has been passed under the provisions of the 1963 Measure. This includes those who have been formally deprived of preferment and declared incapable of holding preferment. Those deposed from Holy Orders are listed. This part of the List also includes those who have signed a Deed of Relinquishment. Each of these is a category of clergy who should be listed and known to bishops when considering new appointments. So we see nothing controversial or disturbing in this part of the List.

5.9   The second part of the List contains the names of clergy under pastoral discipline. The effect of a name being on this part of the List is advisory, not mandatory. However, being listed is unlikely to be helpful for a cleric who is seeking a fresh appointment. In some cases the reason for listing may simply be to highlight the fact that there is a past history that ought to be clearly known to a bishop before he appoints. In other cases it will indicate a cleric whose misdemeanour is sufficiently serious for the archbishop to question whether, for the time being, that cleric should be allowed to exercise his or her Holy Orders.

5.10   The existence of such a List does not surprise us. If such a List did not formally exist, it would undoubtedly exist informally, not least in off-the-record phone calls between relevant parties. The public acknowledgement of the List is, therefore, to be welcomed.

5.11   The problems with the List, which are overwhelmingly to do with the second part, come in three areas.

First, the **secrecy**, which in part has been understandable, is increasingly counter-productive. It creates a breeding ground for wild rumour, for unnecessary misunderstanding, and for nurturing feelings of injustice. So, whilst the content of the List should remain confidential, the more openly understood its existence and procedures become, the better for everyone. Whilst there is more progress to be made here, we would wish to record our appreciation to the Archbishops and their advisers for the progress they have already made in this area.

Secondly, the **types** of misbehaviour or misdemeanour that result in a name being placed on the List give cause for concern. We believe that a large number of the names in the second part should really be in the first part. The reason that this is not so is that, with a reluctance to activate the 1963 Measure procedures, and with the understandable desire to follow 'short cuts' (see paragraphs 3.41 and 8.18), no formal discipline has been exercised. The discipline has been informal, i.e. outside the procedures in the Measure, and so the names cannot be placed in Part 1 of the List. If our proposed new procedures are welcomed, and adhered to by all parties, then this would dramatically reduce the number of names in Part 2, and take away most of the present sense of injustice and disgruntlement.

Thirdly, the **procedure** by which a name is placed upon the List is not well known, nor is it entirely satisfactory at present, although it has been greatly improved in the very recent past. We are concerned that:

(a) there is a lack of consistency among bishops as to what warrants nomination for inclusion on the List. Our understanding is that one bishop might put forward every cleric involved in a divorce, whilst another bishop may never make a nomination in such an instance. Such widely varying practice significantly reduces the overall value of the List, as well as creating a very real measure of injustice, for inclusion on the List appears to have as much to do with the coincidence of diocesan boundaries as it has to do with misdemeanours;

(b) there remains the potential for personal factors, such as a personality clash between bishop and cleric, to weigh too heavily. We have no evidence to allege this has happened, but the procedure is too loose for such a possibility to be ruled out;

(c) the erring cleric is not provided with an adequate opportunity to defend himself before the archbishop places his name on the List. Some clerics may wish to challenge the allegation made by their bishop in proposing them for inclusion on the List. Others may not contest the allegation, but may wish to challenge the bishop's understanding of the details of the matter.

We have been greatly encouraged by more recent improvements in the procedure. The bishop must now inform the cleric of his intention to submit the cleric's name for inclusion on the List. The archbishop now contacts the cleric, indicates the details that have been given concerning him, and invites him to comment. Nevertheless, although this has lengthened the procedure, we feel that the cleric remains at an unacceptably unfair disadvantage:

(a) once on the List, the means of ongoing appeal to have one's case reviewed and removed from the List are relatively unclear. This is not helpful, and can fuel unjustified suspicions that once listed, the name is unlikely to be taken off;

(b)   because of the reservations listed above, the operation of the Caution List could, in some instances, be open to challenge by judicial review. Such a challenge would be harmful to the Church, and to the credibility of the List. So some action needs to be taken, and our outline proposals are listed below.

5.12   Before making our proposals, we would wish to stress that, important though the interests of the individual cleric are, they are not our only concern. The basic philosophy behind the Caution List is the need to protect the Church and society, not least from clergy who are deemed to be inappropriate holders of ecclesiastical office for the time being. This we wish to highlight as a proper concern, and one which must not be dismissed lightly.

5.13   In a number of instances it is clear that the individual cleric sees his position quite differently from the church authorities. No doubt this is inevitable, but the way forward is clear. Given that a cleric has proper opportunity to defend himself, argue his case, and appeal, it must be the Church that ultimately determines who may minister officially in its name. Only the Church can make a determination of acceptable standards for those in Holy Orders. The individual cleric cannot be the arbiter of what is acceptable.

5.14   We propose that the Caution List (probably better entitled 'The Lambeth and Bishopthorpe Register') be formally included in the new Measure. It should be the official record of disciplinary decisions, and any person upon whom a censure is pronounced would be recorded on the List.

5.15   Wherever possible, all disciplinary cases should be handled under the newly proposed procedures. This would transfer the majority of names to Part 1 of the List. The List would record the censure given, and its time span. It would also have a clearly understood appeal procedure for those wishing to have their continued inclusion reviewed.

5.16   Through our proposed tribunal system, the archbishops would be provided with a genuinely independent panel, from whom they could seek advice, and who would hear requests for review and appeals against inclusion.

5.17   Part 2 of the List would then become much smaller. It would cover three ongoing categories of clergy (which, in paragraph 9.22, we suggest might form different 'Parts' of the List):

(a)   Where a cleric voluntarily resigns his office before disciplinary proceedings are invoked, it may still be right to include him on the List. Here, the facts need to be checked. The question to be asked is: had this proceeded through the disciplinary procedure, would a censure have been administered? If the answer is affirmative, it is not unreasonable that a personal resignation should not be allowed to circumvent the discipline that would have been relevant (see paragraph 8.50).

(b)   Where a censure has been exhausted, there might be some offences that still need to have some ongoing record. Child abuse is the obvious example. But it would be unwise to disallow any such provision, especially if there is provided adequate scope for ongoing review (see Chapter 9, paragraph 22).

(c)   It might be appropriate to include a name when no discipline is relevant, but pastoral inadequacy makes it important that bishops should be alerted to enquire in detail before considering appointments.

5.18   The purpose of the List is to protect both Church and society, alerting bishops to whom application is made for appointment of the inappropriateness, at that particular time, of appointing a cleric whose name is on the List. The need is to establish acceptable and detailed procedures which will honour the rules of natural justice. This we believe to be desirable and attainable.

Freeholds and licences

5.19   It is the opinion of the Working Party that the 1963 Measure is distorted in its framing by the need to address freehold. The Working Party has at no point expressed an opinion upon the freehold question. But we are alert to the recent debates in General Synod, and the recommendation of the Steering Group on Clergy Conditions, accepted by Synod, not to proceed at this time with reform of the freehold.

5.20   Our own objective is to frame a disciplinary procedure which is equally applicable to anyone in Holy Orders, whatever the nature of their ecclesiastical office (or lack of office). We have received representations that everyone who is employed by the Church should be included, and notably Lay Workers and Church Army officers. But as our terms of reference are specifically to review 'clergy discipline', we did not feel free to pursue this. We would, however, note in passing that if 'Holy Orders' means anything, there may be areas of answerability that are unique to clergy.

5.21   The most recent figures available in *Numbers in Ministry* (GS Misc 451) tell us that there were 18,749 clergy in the Church of England at the end of 1994. Of these 5,986 are retired (either licensed or with permission to officiate). A further 1,699 are in non-stipendiary or local non-stipendiary ministry. The stipendiary ministry is composed of 615 chaplains employed by non-church organisations, 3,976 who are licensed under seal or are team vicars, and 6,473 who have a freehold (including dignitaries and cathedral staff). So freeholders account for only 34.52 per cent of all the clergy, but 58.50 per cent of the stipendiary clergy.

5.22   Most of the retired clergy who wish to continue ministering do so by seeking from the bishop of the diocese where they reside a Permission to Officiate. This is precisely what it says – a permission to officiate, normally at the invitation of the local incumbent. Discipline is rarely an issue. Ill health and inability to continue to minister are more likely concerns. In such cases, or where such a cleric becomes fractious or uncooperative, the local incumbent simply declines to make use of his services. If problems are more serious it is a simple matter for the bishop to withdraw the Permission to Officiate. If the grounds are disciplinary there might be a case for an appeal against withdrawal.

5.23   The present 1963 Measure is largely designed to address discipline where the complaint is made against a cleric with a freehold office. Our new proposals would be equally applicable to all clergy, whether stipendiary or not, whether active or retired (with or without permission to officiate). Whether the route to be followed in a given case is independent adjudication or voluntary submission to censure by the bishop, the new procedures seek to enshrine the rights of the cleric to be heard and to defend himself if he so wishes.

5.24   The problem area is that of the active clergy, whether stipendiary or not, who do not have a freehold. Those Licensed under Seal are covered by Canon C 12, and it is our opinion that the lack of security offered carries with it the possibility of miscarriages of justice where discipline is involved. Whilst at present beneficed clergy may only be removed from office by following a dauntingly expensive procedure, licensed clergy can be removed very speedily. Those having an indefinite licence may be removed from office on reasonable notice with no right of appeal whatsoever (and with little need for the revocation to be explained). If they have a licence for a fixed term their licence may be summarily revoked, subject only to a right of appeal to the archbishop under Canon C 12.

5.25   Submissions made to us and the personal experience of some of our members led us to conclude that disciplinary offences by licensed clergy are regularly dealt with by revocation of licence in cases where, had the cleric held a freehold office, proceedings under the 1963 Measure would have had to be brought. We speculated on whether, in fact, they would have been brought, and we suspect that in practice discipline is imposed on the licensed clergy in respect of offences for which it would not be imposed on the beneficed clergy. We also believe that there are cases where the easy option of revocation of licence has been chosen where the offence is one which, because of its seriousness, should have been dealt with by proceedings under the 1963 Measure.

5.26   There is a huge disparity between the considerable security of tenure which beneficed clergy enjoy and the lack of security experienced by licensed clergy.   We do not see it as our task to accept this disparity where the issue involved is one of discipline. We are not able to recommend a system which would make it easier to proceed against beneficed clergy whilst retaining the present insecurity of licensed clergy.

5.27   In no way do we wish to interfere with the bishop's unfettered discretion concerning who should and who should not be given a licence. That must remain a matter for the bishop alone. We also accept that there are grounds on which a licence under seal should terminate which are quite unconnected with matters of discipline – for example, the curate at the end of his curacy, or the priest in charge when pastoral reorganisation is completed and a new incumbent is to be instituted. Here again, we would not wish to interfere in any way with the bishop's existing discretion. But where the grounds for revocation are disciplinary, then we believe that adjustments need to be made.

5.28   We therefore make the following recommendations.

(a)   **Fixed term licence** We recommend that the present system should be retained, whereby there is no right of appeal or review if a fixed term licence expires upon its completion and is not renewed. However, we recommend that during the fixed term, the licence should not be revocable by the bishop on notice as it is at present. Ecclesiastical offences committed by licensed clergy should be dealt with in the same way as offences by freehold clergy. Removal from office (which would include revocation of licence) should be a penalty open to the tribunal hearing the complaint, or the bishop in cases where a penalty is imposed by consent.

(b)   **Expired fixed term licence** We are aware of instances where fixed term licences expire and nothing is done to renew them. However, the cleric continues to exercise his ministry unchallenged by the bishop. We believe that provision must be made to introduce a measure of certainty here. We therefore recommend that where a cleric continues in office after the expiry of a fixed term licence, unless the bishop has, prior to the licence's expiring, requested the cleric to vacate his office, the bishop shall be required to give three months' notice to terminate the appointment. We also recommend that if the cleric continues in office for more than twelve months after expiry of the licence without the bishop serving notice within that period, the licence shall become an indefinite licence.

(c)   **Indefinite licence** We consider that, wherever practicable, there is good sense in making a licence for a fixed term, even if this is for a brief period. But where a licence is indefinite we recommend that the bishop should still use the disciplinary procedure, rather than take the apparently 'easy route' of giving three months' notice of intention to revoke. When issuing the licence the bishop should be able to specify one or more prescribed grounds on which the licence may be terminated, and then give notice of his revocation on such prescribed grounds. These could include the situations where the licence is as a priest in charge, where a pastoral scheme comes into effect, or where suspension of presentation is lifted. If such specified events occur the licence will terminate on notice given. Other pastoral reasons might arise unforeseen at the time of granting the licence. In such cases nothing is lost by giving the reasons when revoking the licence.

Where the grounds for revocation are of a disciplinary nature then we would wish to insist that the disciplinary procedure be followed. Failure to do this can significantly diminish the rights of the cleric to challenge the allegation. It also means that discipline is administered without the Church having the ongoing protection that is provided by a record of the censure on Part 1 of the Caution List.

Codes of Practice

5.29   In providing an essentially flexible procedure that will be relevant to a wide range of potential cases, and which will prove both practicable and durable, it is important to distinguish between what can be established by Measure, and what should be more readily amendable (see Chapter 3, paragraph 40).

5.30   We suggest the proposed new Measure should enact our proposals in Chapters 6 to 9 of this Report. The Measure should also require Codes of Practice to be formulated to guide those responsible for exercising discipline. These Codes should be under regular review by the Clergy Disciplinary Commission (see Chapter 7), who would be responsible for tabling modifications to the Codes in the light of experience. Such amendments would require the consent of the General Synod. The Church would wish to be confident that the guidelines in the Code of Practice were being followed. Where a case is forwarded for independent adjudication, the Tribunal would expect that the Codes of Practice had been adhered to in the preliminary stages. Equally, a cleric could appeal against censure by consent if he could demonstrate that the bishop had disregarded the Codes of Practice and the cleric had been prejudiced thereby.

Hearings in public or in private?

5.31   One of the major criticisms of the 1963 Measure has been the publicity that cases reaching the Consistory Court engender. This has been viewed as damaging and detrimental to the Church and its mission. It can also be unduly injurious to the cleric concerned, whether adjudged guilty or innocent. Being in the glare of publicity can be prejudicial when seeking a fresh appointment.

5.32   It has to be recognised that erring clerics, like erring doctors, are a source of media interest. Equally, an erring cleric is, inevitably, bad news for the Church. Where the press unearth wrongdoing by investigative journalism, this is a service for which the Church is grateful, as it focuses on a situation where the Church would wish to respond. The only safe remedy is a situation in which no cleric falls short of the expected standards! Exposing wrongdoing is part of the service that the press offer the public and the Church. But they tend to focus more specifically upon some areas of discipline (morals, sexual behaviour and financial irregularity) whilst showing little interest in other areas of discipline.

5.33   Given the right of the media to investigate and expose where they can, it still remains to be considered whether a disciplinary hearing should be open to the public, or held in private.

● In favour of **public** hearings is the need for transparency. There can be no suggestion of hiding away dirty linen when all can listen in if they wish.

- However, **non-public** hearings do not offend against the principle of transparency, so long as proper procedures are meticulously followed. The media have no greater 'right' to know than any member of the general public. What the Church and society most need is assurance that discipline is not being shirked, but is being responsibly exercised.

By excluding the public, a hearing may be less emotionally charged, witnesses may be more willing to testify, the truth may be more accurately assessed and the future possibilities of reconciliation and restoration may be enhanced. Whilst there may be incidental publicity anyway, less opportunity may be afforded for gratuitous publicity.

5.34 The various arguments are finely balanced. Our proposal is that disciplinary hearings will not normally be open to the public, but the adjudication reached will invariably be made in public. However, we would recommend that the defence (i.e. the accused cleric) may request the hearing to be in public, giving reasons for this request. Also, the chairman of the tribunal may, exceptionally, direct a public hearing where it is perceived that the interests of the Church would be best served, as, for instance, in some cases of doctrinal discipline.

Political opinions

5.35 Section 14(1) of the 1963 Measure protects clergy against disciplinary proceedings in respect of their political opinions or activities. No doubt this proviso is historically to be understood in the context of the post-war situation, and the fact of Eastern European Communism.

5.36 We would wish to retain the protection of political *opinion*. But political *activity* needs to be restricted by two provisos. Political activity that breaks the laws of our land should not be protected, and conviction in a criminal court should not be set aside on this defence. Equally, a cleric (especially one with a stipend) is expected to fulfil the requirements of his office. Failure to do so, or neglect of duties because of time and attention given to political activity, would not be a defence against disciplinary charges.

Grievance procedures

5.37   One representation that we received from several correspondents was the absence of a grievance procedure in the Church of England. It was argued that alongside a reformed disciplinary system there should be means for a cleric to voice a grievance when his affairs had been mishandled.

5.38   Most professions now have a grievance procedure which forms a mirror to the disciplinary system. People in positions of authority do sometimes make mistakes, through human failure or ignorance. When mistakes are made those in positions of seniority do not always, for understandable reasons, find it easy to admit to error. This can lead to frustration and ill-will amongst clergy, who are often wary of appealing over the head of an archdeacon to the bishop, or over the head of the bishop to the archbishop.

5.39   We had sympathy for the representations made to us. However, we felt that grievance procedures were outside our terms of reference. So we consulted the Clergy Conditions of Service Steering Group, and Appendix C at the end of this Report outlines a procedure that might be appropriate if the General Synod considered a Grievance Procedure to be helpful.

Problems of ignorance

5.40   The present disciplinary procedure is poorly understood. Few clergy would be able to explain the procedure to be followed were a complaint to be laid against them. Nor would the Diocesan Registrar be an appropriate source of guidance, as the Registrar would be advising the bishop, and organising the Consistory Court to hear the complaint! Equally, many bishops and archdeacons remain unclear of the detail. Diocesan Registrars are more aware in theory, but vary markedly in the practical experience they have had in disciplinary cases. Diocesan Chancellors cannot be consulted in the early stages of a complaint, as it will be their responsibility to preside over the Consistory Court hearing that could result. As only three cases have gone that far in 32 years, very few Chancellors have any first hand experience of the present procedures.

5.41   The proposed new procedures should be very much simpler to understand. Just as many employees receive information on the disciplinary arrangements relevant to their employment, when first they commence work, so we consider that it would be helpful for all ordinands to receive a simple explanation of the church's disciplinary procedures, in pamphlet form, before they are ordained. Given the acceptance of our proposals by the General Synod, it might be appropriate for such an information pamphlet to be circulated to all serving clergy once the new Measure is in use.

5.42   A second area of ignorance that might need to be addressed is the ignorance among clergy of what is expected of them. Relatively few clergy appear to be conversant with the 'Canons of the Church of England'. Such an information pamphlet as is suggested in the previous paragraph might also highlight the need to read through the Canons, and indicate the standards generally expected of the clergy of the Church of England.

Personnel matters in the Church of England

5.43   Discipline is, we are aware, but one part, albeit a very important part, of a wider picture. In the Church of England there is no personnel department to bring together the various parties. There are no tribunals to which appeal can be made against wrongful dismissal and no independent procedures for handling grievances. Appraisal structures are in an early stage of development. Most clergy are not in a trade union to provide support when under threat.

5.44   Our proposals with regard to discipline are, therefore, made on their own merits. But we would hope that they might also be contributory to the development of a wider set of personnel arrangements, the need for which has already been highlighted by the Clergy Conditions of Service Steering Group. Meanwhile, all clergy need proper safeguards, and to feel confident that the procedures established are fair and just and will protect them against arbitrary and prejudiced judgements.

6

THE SCOPE OF DISCIPLINE

6.1   It is our view that clerical discipline should apply to all who are in Holy Orders in the Church of England. The 10,500 in ministry for which the Church directly pays the stipend are those we first think of when discussing discipline. But there are also over 600 clergy serving a secular employer (e.g. as chaplains in prisons, hospitals, schools and the armed forces), and a substantial number of non-stipendiary clergy. Additionally, there are over 5,000 who are retired, but who continue to serve, holding a licence or the bishop's Permission to Officiate. Some few fall outside all these categories, but continue to style themselves 'Reverend' and to benefit from their perceived status as clergy.

6.2   All of these have been episcopally ordained and set apart for ministry. They have all, at their ordination, made and subscribed to the Declaration of Assent and the Oath of Canonical Obedience. Failure to do so would have prevented their ordination, their varied preferments, and their current standing as clergy in the Church of England.

6.3   However, although representations were made to us to widen the scope of discipline still further, we do not recommend the inclusion of deaconesses, Church Army officers, other licensed lay workers, or readers. There may well be cogent arguments to review disciplinary procedures for each of these groups. But to join them with those in Holy Orders would be unhelpful and confusing.

A rich diversity

6.4   It is from the Church, through the bishop, that the clergy receive their authority to minister. That authority is only given where the cleric commits himself to serve within the broad parameters of what the Church at any moment in its history deems to be appropriate and acceptable.

6.5   Within the Church of England those parameters are deliberately set broadly. The Church allows for considerable diversity of expression and practice. On a range of ethical issues it does not demand detailed compliance to one position. On doctrinal matters a width of interpretation is tolerated, and felt to be acceptable if we are to tease out and clarify the tenets of the Faith and their implications for godly living.

6.6   Yet, whilst diversity is expected and encouraged, that diversity is still to be exercised within the boundaries acceptable to the Christian community. As will be seen in the New Testament records, those boundaries will from time to time be re-evaluated and adjusted in the light of growing understanding. In Acts 15, for instance, adjustments are discussed in the light of Gentiles becoming part of the faith community. Such reassessments have continued ever since. It was in this way, for example, that over the centuries the Church's position on slavery eventually moved from acquiescence to opposition.

6.7   We do not see it as within our remit to identify where the acceptable boundaries are to be set in the contemporary church. What we seek to offer is a reformed structure and procedure for the Church to use when those boundaries are breached, a structure that is not only flexible yet fair in responding to breaches, but which is also equally applicable to all allegations of a cleric's falling short of the required minimum for acceptability.

Existing ecclesiastical offences

6.8   Disciplinary procedures are required where an 'ecclesiastical offence' is being alleged. We use this term deliberately, to distinguish what we are addressing from other types of offence. The Tyler and Lincoln cases (see Chapter 1) both engendered confusion in many people, who saw a charge of adultery appearing to be treated as a criminal offence, when in secular law it is not criminal.

6.9   The confusion arose because the Consistory Court is modelled, for its procedure in adjudicating, upon the Crown Court. Our proposals in Chapter 7 will, we hope, seek to remove this confusion.

For whatever the procedure deemed to be appropriate, the offences being considered by the Church are breaches of approved standards within its own community. Only in a few instances will this be mirrored by a similar concern in the secular community.

6.10   The ecclesiastical offences that require a disciplinary procedure, to determine whether a cleric has fallen short and to respond to his guilt being established, are found in the 1963 Measure. They are listed in two separate sections:

Section 14 – ecclesiastical offences, which may be:

- against the laws ecclesiastical involving matters of doctrine, ritual or ceremonial;

- conduct unbecoming the office and work of a clerk in Holy Orders;

- serious, persistent, or continuous neglect of duty.

Section 55 – a range of decisions reached in the secular courts which it is considered are incompatible with holding preferment in the Church of England. These include:

- conviction for a criminal offence where imprisonment is the sentence (whether suspended or not);

- divorce, where the clergy spouse relied upon adultery, desertion, or unreasonable behaviour in the cleric when bringing the petition;

- a finding of having committed adultery in a matrimonial cause;

- an affiliation order having been made against the cleric;

- wilful neglect to maintain spouse or children when an order has been made against the cleric.

We would propose that all potential grounds for disciplinary action should, in the new Measure, be collected together in the same section.

6.11   The 1963 Measure places most discipline under the phrase '*conduct unbecoming the office and work of a clerk in Holy Orders*'. We have noticed with interest that most recent disciplinary reforms in other provinces of the Anglican Communion have tended to move away from this generalised and non-specific terminology, to list offences in greater detail.

6.12   We found ourselves in some sympathy with this trend. Whilst a more specific statement of offences risks becoming too rigid and exclusive, it does assist in clarifying what sorts of behaviour are acceptable or unacceptable. So we have attempted to offer a few more tightly worded offences, whilst retaining something of the older wording to allow for offences that might otherwise become excluded.

6.13   The Scriptures teach us that it is a Christian duty to support the governing authorities, especially in their maintenance of law and order. Romans 13. 1-7 is quite clear that the *'governing authorities'* are *'to bring punishment on the wrong-doer.'* So we would wish to emphasise that one part of the Church of England's disciplinary procedures is to assist and co-operate with the civil authorities when they seek to investigate crimes or alleged illegalities. Our longstanding acceptance of a finding of guilt in a criminal court as sufficient proof of a wrongdoing (section 55 of the 1963 Measure) must carry with it a corresponding willingness to assist the secular authorities in their enquiries that precede a decision to prosecute. It is never justifiable to withhold evidence from police enquiries. Nor is it right to shield a cleric in order to avoid a criminal prosecution, or to assume that the Church should or can deal internally and privately with a criminal allegation. But equally, it is just as important that a cleric should be offered support, advice and assistance to mount a proper defence, for it is not unknown for clergy to be the subject of false allegations.

6.14   In clarifying the range of ecclesiastical offences, we reflect the responsibilities and privileges of those in Holy Orders, as set out in Chapter 3 (paragraphs 25 to 27) of this Report. As we state there, the ecclesiastical offences clarify what is expected of clergy, and what will constitute an unacceptable falling short of that expectation. The statement of ecclesiastical offences also exists to reassure the church community, and the surrounding society, that clergy are not free to 'do their own thing', and that, to protect the Christian community and society generally, where a cleric is found to have committed one or more of these offences, disciplinary action will be forthcoming.

Future ecclesiastical offences

WILFUL DISOBEDIENCE TO OR BREACH OF THE LAWS ECCLESIASTICAL

6.15   For the Church of England there is a range of legally established rules. These are found as Canons of the Church of England and in various Measures. Both the Canons and the Measures have an applicability wider than just the clergy. But the clergy are required to conduct themselves within the rules set down, and, upon ordination or appointment, publicly commit themselves so to do. For instance, they state in their Oath of Obedience their willingness only to use forms of service authorised or allowed by Canon. This category of ecclesiastical offence would include ritual and ceremonial offences.

NEGLECT, CULPABLE CARELESSNESS OR GROSS INEFFICIENCY IN THE PERFORMANCE OF THE DUTIES OF THEIR OFFICE

6.16   In any other profession, if you fail to do your job properly, then inevitably, and however sadly, it means that you will not be able to practise in the profession, with all the attendant loss that follows. Whilst on occasions we may have sympathy with those who fail to do their job properly, both the general public and the church need to be protected. With great privileges and great trust go greater responsibility. This is echoed in *Clergy Conditions of Service* (GS 1126), with its concern for the 'pastorally inadequate'. People need priests and they need the comfort of the Church's ministry. If that comfort and example are not forthcoming the damage done is just as great as if a solicitor or doctor or nurse does not perform his or her duty. We would suggest that, unlike the 1963 Measure (see paragraphs 5.35 and 36), the defence of political activity should not be allowed where neglect, carelessness or gross inefficiency is the allegation.

CONDUCT INAPPROPRIATE OR UNBECOMING THE OFFICE AND WORK OF A CLERK IN HOLY ORDERS

6.17   As we saw in Chapter 3, it is not unreasonable for Christians to model their life on that of their clergy (cf. Hebrews 13.7), and for society to view clergy as representative and consistent examples of Christian behaviour.

TEACHING, PREACHING, PUBLISHING OR PROFESSING DOCTRINE OR BELIEF INCOMPATIBLE WITH THAT OF THE CHURCH OF ENGLAND AS EXPRESSED WITHIN ITS CREEDS AND FORMULARIES

6.18   Belief is central in a Christian church and the Church of England is founded upon the teachings of the Scriptures, the ancient Creeds and its historic formularies. Our clergy are called upon to make a clear and consistent reiteration of the essentials of the faith. The Church of England represents a breadth of theological approach. It has been described as having a hard central core (represented by the Scriptures and the Creeds), and a less clear-cut, more fuzzy circumference. If this is so, and if the Declaration of Assent taken by all in Holy Orders is to have any meaning, then there must be a limit to the breadth of doctrinal expression. Denial of the central core must be excluded if the community of faith is to retain any distinctiveness. This is not to suggest a denial of free speech, simply to insist that some doctrinal positions are inconsistent with being an authorised guardian or teacher of the church.

CONVICTION IN A SECULAR COURT OF AN OFFENCE FOR WHICH A SENTENCE OF IMPRISONMENT CAN BE GIVEN

6.19   The finding of guilt in the secular court shall be sufficient proof in and of itself. Where prison is the result, the response of the Church will usually have to be removal from office. But where a suspended prison sentence or a lesser secular penalty is imposed, the Church should retain flexibility in determining what ecclesiastical response is appropriate in each case.

6.20   The category outlined under paragraph 17 above is sufficient to cover matrimonial and family issues. However, it will probably be important, in maintaining the Church of England's clear position that lifelong monogamous marriage is God's creative intent, to make it clear that certain situations are thereby incompatible with the exercise of Holy Orders. These are:

- being found to have committed adultery in a matrimonial cause

- having an affiliation order made against a cleric

- being found guilty of wilful neglect as a party to a marriage to maintain the other party or child/children of the family (section 27 of the Matrimonial Causes Act of 1973).

6.21   The 1963 Measure makes deprivation automatic for any cleric where his marriage is declared irretrievably broken, the evidence provided being his adultery, unreasonable behaviour or desertion. Under the newly enacted Family Law Act of 1996, where 'fault' no longer needs to be alleged to justify that a marriage is irretrievably broken, the 1963 Measure will have to be reframed, as the provision is now outdated.

6.22   It would seem reasonable and wise to require a mandatory review by the Church whenever a cleric is involved in divorce or a judicial separation. Where the grounds listed in the last paragraph are found to be part of the breakdown of the marital relationship, then this should continue to be seen as a disciplinary matter. The Church of England still upholds the lifelong nature of the marriage vows, and so a falling short in this area by clergy (who also officiate at the wedding ceremony when such vows are entered into) must continue to be a very real cause for concern.

6.23   As this Report is to precede the detailed draft legislation required to bring it into effect, we invite the General Synod to affirm, add to, or reduce the range of ecclesiastical offences that we have suggested. Very great care will be needed in drafting the legislation at this point. But this chapter outlines the offences we propose should be included.

6.24   Representations have been made for offences additional to those we have suggested above. We gave particular attention to the suggestion that there should be an offence of 'bringing the Church into disrepute'. It was suggested to us that there might be instances where a cleric was, technically, fulfilling his responsibilities, but in such a way as to be distasteful or to create public and open scandal. The occasional poor relationship between an incumbent and his curate was one example cited to us. Whilst we had some sympathy for what was being asked for, we concluded that such a category of offence was too wide, and, therefore, open to abuse. As Canon C 26.2 requires a cleric 'at all times [to] be diligent to frame and fashion his life . . . according to the doctrine of Christ, and to make himself [a] wholesome example and pattern to the flock of Christ', we felt that such sad situations were covered by paragraphs 15 and 17 above and so did not require separate provision to be made for them.

7

THE CORE STRUCTURES

Developing a new procedure

7.1   As has been seen in Chapter 2, the 1963 Measure prescribes essentially four different procedures depending on whether a complaint is against a priest or deacon or an archbishop or bishop, and whether it relates to their conduct or involves doctrine, ritual or ceremonial. All but one of these procedures involve both a preliminary legal hearing and a trial. With the exception of conduct complaints against a priest or deacon, all of the procedures require the formation of exceptionally high-powered tribunals. For example, the preliminary hearing of a conduct complaint against a bishop would involve a committee comprising an archbishop, two diocesan bishops and a legal assessor. Trial would be before a Commission of Convocation comprising the Dean of the Arches and four diocesan bishops. An appeal would be heard by three Lords of Appeal in Ordinary and two Bishops with a seat in the House of Lords. The complete procedure would therefore involve eight diocesan bishops and one archbishop.

7.2   We have noted that the procedure for trial of a conduct complaint against a priest or deacon has been used on only three occasions since the 1963 Measure came into force. The evidence which we have received suggests that the Measure is seen very much as an instrument of last resort to be used only where less formal methods (such as resignation or revocation of licence and the Caution List) cannot be used. We believe that the procedures for any other type of complaint are so unwieldy and expensive that it is almost inconceivable that they would ever be used.

7.3   We have sought to produce a more simplified system which would enable all disciplinary complaints, whether or not they would result in a formal trial, to be dealt with within a single procedure. Our objective has been to produce a system which would enable discipline to be dealt with in an open and consistent manner in a way which is fair to the accused but affordable to the Church.

7.4   The system of discipline that we are proposing is new, both in the structures that will be needed, and in the procedures that will be followed. In this chapter we examine the structures that we propose and in Chapter 8 we shall outline the procedures that we propose should be followed.

A new forum: The Clergy Discipline Tribunal

7.5   We recommend that all disciplinary cases where an adjudication is needed should be tried by a new tribunal which we have termed the Clergy Discipline Tribunal. This would replace the Consistory Court and the Court of Ecclesiastical Causes Reserved in discipline (but not, of course, faculty) matters, and would also replace the Commission of Convocation for trying complaints against bishops. There is no magic in the use of the word 'tribunal' as opposed to 'court'. We envisage that tribunal hearings would be conducted with slightly less formality than hearings in the Consistory Court, but the principal difference would be that the members·of the Tribunal would hear a case as a tribunal rather than with the judge and jury demarcation which exists between the Chancellor and Assessors in the Consistory Court. The scope for technical challenges (for example through a misdirection of the Assessors) would thereby be reduced.

7.6   We believe that the Tribunal should be established on a national basis, although we accept that it would be equally workable (although possibly more expensive) if it were to operate on a provincial basis. We believe, however, that it is imperative that the Tribunal and its members and officers should be unconnected with the diocese from which the complaint arises, although the hearing should take place at a venue convenient to the parties. We believe also that the Tribunal should be independent of the central structures of the Church, particularly in the light of the recommendations which we make below about the manner in which complaints should be prosecuted.

7.7   The workload of the Tribunal is an unknown quantity. The procedures for trial in the 1963 Measure came to be regarded with such disfavour that many of the cases for which the procedure was designed were never dealt with under it. We would expect more cases to be referred to the Tribunal, and it will have other functions (see Chapter 8). So we expect a modest increase in its use. We do not recommend that the Tribunal should be established with a permanent office and a full-time dedicated staff. Instead, we believe that the Tribunal could function initially with only two permanent officers, both part-time: an overall chairman or President and a registrar.

7.8   The President would be appointed by the archbishops in consultation with the Dean of the Arches and would be required to have a seven years general legal qualification or to have held high judicial office (these being the qualifications required for a diocesan chancellor). The functions of the President would include issuing practice directions to ensure the smooth working of the Tribunal, dealing with interlocutory matters such as suspension orders and striking out malicious or vexatious complaints, and also chairing tribunal hearings, perhaps where important points of law or principle were involved. We envisage that the President would be offered a retainer, perhaps equal to the annual fee for the Vicar-General of the Province of Canterbury.

7.9   The day to day administration of the Tribunal would be undertaken by the registrar who could also, with the consent of the President, deal with minor interlocutory matters such as the issuing of directions where they were required in a case. It may be most cost effective for the registrar to be a lawyer in private practice, who already has the necessary office facilities and support staff to service the work of the Tribunal and who could be paid an inclusive retainer.

7.10   When a Tribunal needed to be constituted to hear a particular case it would be chaired by a chairman appointed by the President from a panel drawn up by the Dean of the Arches in consultation with the Clergy Discipline Commission (see paragraph 7.15 below). Persons eligible to be on the panel of chairmen would be communicant members of the Church of England with a seven years general legal qualification and legal experience in areas particularly appropriate to disciplinary hearings.

7.11   The chairman would sit with two other members: one clerical and one lay, each appointed from panels drawn up by the Commission. The panel of clergy would be of those who have been in Holy Orders for a minimum of ten years. The panel of lay people would be from those who are communicants in good standing. Some of our members who are, for example, magistrates would be eminently suitable; but the panel would look more widely than this, and would reflect gender, ethnic and other groupings in its overall makeup.

7.12   All three panels would have a membership widely distributed over the whole country. Whilst no panel member would ever hear a case concerning a cleric in their home diocese, the intention is for hearings to be held locally, using panel members from the region where possible. Because the hearings would be less formal and more private, we envisage the use of appropriate church owned buildings, of which the Church of England has a wide variety in every part of the country. All these factors should assist in moderating costs, whilst enhancing convenience, reducing delay, yet maintaining justice.

7.13   We have suggested a tribunal of three members, which is widely used in both the magistrates' courts and in the appellate courts of our land.

(a)   On points of law the Tribunal would defer to the ruling of the chairman.

(b)   On questions of fact, guilt or innocence and decisions about penalties, all decisions would be by majority, each with an equal voice.

(c)   In cases involving ceremonial, ritual or doctrine, we suggest that the case be referred to the House of Bishops (to that House's Theological Committee) for their observations prior to the hearing. The House of Bishops would also appoint two suitably qualified assessors to advise the Tribunal when the hearing takes place.

We would suggest that members of a Tribunal should be entitled to be paid their expenses. Whilst we are aware of suitably qualified lawyers who would happily volunteer a day or an afternoon to chair a Tribunal at no cost to the Church other than expenses, we would suggest that chairmen be able to claim a prescribed fee for their services if they so wished.

7.14   The procedure of the Tribunal would be governed by rules designed to ensure that the principles of natural justice were observed. We recommend that the standard of proof on the complaint should continue to be proof beyond reasonable doubt.

A new national Commission: The Clergy Discipline Commission

7.15   We perceive the need for a central standing body to oversee the discipline process and we therefore recommend the establishment of a permanent Commission whose members would be appointed (under the present system) by the Standing Committee or (if the reforms recommended by the Turnbull Commission are implemented) the Appointments Committee. The members would be appointed from amongst the members of General Synod, and would include people with particular skills and experience. They would be unpaid, but there would be a professional secretariat provided by Church House staff.

7.16   The Commission would be responsible for maintaining lists of suitable lay and clergy members for the Tribunal and lists of investigators (see paragraph 7.19 below), and the Commission would also advise bishops on the imposition of a penalty by consent, and review cases where a bishop had decided not to take formal disciplinary action. The Commission would also formulate the necessary Codes of Practice and issue general policy guidance. Where the Codes of Practice are seen to be in need of amendment the Commission would consult widely, formulate proposals and then lay these before the General Synod for approval. The Commission would produce a regular report to General Synod.

7.17   We believe that the costs to the Church of the Commission would be minimal. It would probably need to meet in full no more than four times a year and would be able to delegate certain of its functions, such as advising bishops, to a small sub-committee.

7.18   Part of the necessary reforms must be to avoid a proliferation of bodies dealing with disciplinary procedure. To this end we looked very closely at combining the existing Legal Aid Commission with the proposed Clergy Discipline Commission. The proposal initially appeared attractive, but on further investigation we propose to leave the Legal Aid Commission in its present form. It must be remembered that the Legal Aid Commission deals more widely than just with discipline. Because the clergy are not among the more affluent members of the community, ecclesiastical legal aid is rarely refused on the grounds that the applicant could afford legal advice and representation without legal aid. This is a delicate area, involving assessment of a cleric's financial resources, and whether the applicant has reasonable grounds for taking, defending, or being party to the proceedings. It is important that this assessment should be undertaken by persons wholly and clearly separate from the prosecuting body. Our proposals include the provision of time limits within which, in normal circumstances, various stages of the disciplinary procedures must be completed. We were concerned at the possibility that leaving the decision on the grant of legal aid with the Commission might contribute to delays in dealing with disciplinary cases. But the new Legal Aid Rules which were approved in 1995 give the Secretary to the Legal Aid Commission increased powers to grant interim legal aid before the Commission as a whole is able to meet. Furthermore, our information is that the Legal Aid Commission can and does meet at a few days' notice where necessary.

The legal department

7.19   We refer throughout this chapter to 'the legal department'. By this we have in mind the Legal Services Department which may flow from the recommendations of the Turnbull Report; but if the recommendations of that Report were not implemented the functions could nevertheless be carried out under the auspices of the General Synod Office, although some augmentation in staff would be required. The function of the legal department in our system would be to act as prosecutor in discipline cases. The legal department would consider cases referred to it, decide whether the allegations disclosed an ecclesiastical offence, appoint an investigator to collect the evidence, oversee the investigation, consider the evidence and decide whether prosecution was justified and, if it was, issue the proceedings and have the conduct of the prosecution. It might be an advantage if the staff of the legal department included at least one lawyer with experience of advocacy. We believe that by centralising prosecutions in this way there would be a consistency in practice, and the costs would be lower than if the bishops were required to engage local lawyers to prosecute each case.

Investigators

7.20   A national system for prosecution can only work if there is a national network of persons able to investigate alleged offences and collect evidence in an appropriate form. We recommend that the Commission be responsible for drawing up a list of suitably experienced people across the country to investigate alleged offences and gather evidence. We envisage that they would require some formal training, but they would volunteer their services without charge and would only be paid their expenses. We do not prescribe the type of person who may be suitable to fulfil this role. A serving or retired archdeacon or rural dean may be appropriate where the complaint arises in a neighbouring diocese, but we believe that there will be many lay people (such as retired police officers) with the appropriate skills. We would cite diocesan visitors (under 'Broken Rites') as an example of the willingness of people to give their time in the service of the Church.

Diocesan resources

7.21   No new resources are being proposed within each diocese. However, because the Consistory Court will no longer be used for discipline cases, and as no case will be heard by personnel from within the diocese of the accused cleric, both the Diocesan Registrar and the Diocesan Chancellor will be freed to be advisers to the bishop as and when he requires their help. The bishop may also wish to make use of those within his diocese who serve on Tribunal panels. As they will never be used to adjudicate within their own diocese, they may come to be a valuable advisory resource to their bishop.

7.22   What many dioceses and bishops may need to review are their current practices with regard to record keeping. Much can be learned from other professions and disciplinary procedures involving simple, yet accurate and reliable note taking of interviews and telephone conversations. Especially in the case of interviews, it is always helpful if a copy of the notes can be provided for the cleric and for the cleric to agree that it is an accurate summary (see paragraph 3.44).

Caution List

7.23   This will continue to be kept at Lambeth and Bishopthorpe. It will continue to be circulated after updating to diocesan and area bishops on the current strictly confidential basis. However, we hope that the overwhelming majority of names included will be for recognised disciplinary offences recorded after due process.

7.24   Clergy should have the right to know whether their name is on the List and to know what is recorded against their name. They should be free to challenge both their inclusion and the information about them that is recorded.

- If they are included following due disciplinary process, it is to the Tribunal that they would make their appeal, as the archbishops cannot be expected to override the disciplinary procedure.

- If they are included outside of the disciplinary procedure, then the present system of nomination by the diocesan bishop will have taken place, with appropriate notice to the cleric by the archbishop. In such cases it will be to the archbishop that appeal is made, but the archbishop should be free to refer the matter to the Tribunal if he considers that this would assist. Once the archbishop has made such a referral, then both that appeal, and any subsequent appeals, shall be to the Tribunal.

Should not ceremonial, ritual and doctrine cases be kept separate?

7.25   In cases involving doctrine the newly worded offence (see Chapter 6, paragraph 18) allows for such discipline. The Church of

England is a confessional church. By this we mean that it holds to a central core of essential beliefs, expressed in the Scriptures, the Creeds and its historic formularies. Discipline of the clergy would be incomplete without this category. But it is provided only for the exercise of discipline. It is not a vehicle for establishing what the beliefs of the Church of England are. A disciplinary court would be both inappropriate and dangerous for such an exploration. But we do not see the need for a separate procedure or a separate adjudication panel.

7.26   Similarly, in cases involving ceremonial and ritual, the offence outlined in Chapter 6, paragraph 15 covers such cases. The present elaborate provision through the Court of Ecclesiastical Causes Reserved has been little used and is complicated to understand. So we see the referral to the House of Bishops and the provision of two assessors (paragraph 7.13 (c) above), as also in doctrine cases, to be adequate.

8

THE CORE PROCEDURES

8.1   Whilst disciplinary cases are relatively few in number, it would be misleading to presume that there have been only three cases in 33 years. Only three cases have reached a Consistory Court, which (excluding the appeals process) is the final stage in the procedure provided in the 1963 Measure. Other cases will have been dismissed by the Bishop or the Examiner. Some have proceeded under Censure by Consent or by revocation of licence. Others have been resolved less formally, or by the voluntary (or encouraged!) resignation of the cleric. But throughout there has been a marked and growing resistance to using the court part of the procedure and this has, inevitably, distorted the system.

8.2   We have sought to learn from the reality of current practice. Where possible, we have built the new procedures on those parts of current practice that are workable and appropriate. Many disciplinary situations are neither of major gravity, nor do they need a formal trial. Our objective has been to produce a system which will enable discipline to be dealt with in an open and consistent manner; in a way that is fair to the accused yet affordable to the Church; which is understandable and undelayed; and which permits the bishop to oversee the procedure without adding directly to his personal workload.

How practicable are the new proposals?

8.3   Bearing in mind that the 1963 Measure has failed to provide a satisfactory and enduring way forward in discipline cases, we acknowledge the need not only to offer our new way forward, but also to consider the practicality of our proposals. Will the new proposed procedure work any more satisfactorily than that which it seeks to replace?

8.4   Ultimately, that is a question that cannot be answered. By its very nature, proposed ecclesiastical legislation of this sort cannot be 'road-tested' in a controlled experiment prior to being enacted. So, as with much legislation, only time will answer the question. However, bearing this caveat in mind, we do nevertheless present our proposals with a considerable degree of confidence as to their practicality and as to their appropriateness for the Church of England, both now and for some length of time to come.

8.5   We have been able to review what in reality actually happens in the Church of England at present. We have received a lot of representations. We have been able to observe the same process being undertaken by other Anglican Provinces and by several other Churches. Alongside this we have drawn on the experience of several of the professions in their disciplinary procedures, and reviewed the lessons to be learned from tribunals, many of which postdate the 1963 Measure.

Making a complaint

8.6   The 1963 Measure only becomes operational, even for censure by consent, once an appropriately worded complaint is lodged in the diocesan registry. This is, of itself, a disincentive to activate the formal disciplinary procedure. In the case of parishioners, a minimum of six members of the Electoral Roll must put their name to this formal complaint.

8.7   We believe that making a complaint should not be surrounded by excessive formality. It should be in writing, but initially a simple letter should be sufficient, so long as the nature of the complaint is clear. The complaint may come through the bishop's own staff, from parishes (through PCCs and Churchwardens), or from individuals.

8.8   Once a written complaint is received by the bishop, we propose a maximum period of four weeks, within which the complaint will go through a filtering process, and a decision on what further progress, if any, needs to be taken. The bishop would delegate responsibility to check out the complaint to whomsoever he felt suitable, such as an archdeacon, rural dean, registrar or lay person.

During this initial exploration it would be:

- the responsibility of the complainant to clarify and amplify the complaint they have made, providing evidence to substantiate their allegation;

- the responsibility of the bishop's appointed investigator to listen to the complainant, and also the cleric (if the cleric wishes to comment at this stage). It is important that complaints that are frivolous, maliciously motivated, or without substance, are disposed of quickly.

8.9   In many cases this initial investigation will be completed in a matter of days. The suggestion of four weeks is to prevent delays developing, and is seen as the longest allowable time before the bishop makes his first decision, based upon the report provided by his initial investigator. By this means we are bringing the bishop into potential disciplinary matters right from the beginning. In the light of what is already happening in terms of complaints made to the bishop, one of four responses will conclude this initial consideration of the complaint:

(a)   If it is seen as frivolous, malicious or unsubstantiated, the bishop will dismiss the complaint.

(b)   If the complaint is obviously of a serious nature, then the bishop would follow the formal procedures straight away. Some cases would be handled under the Incumbents (Vacation of Benefices) Measures procedures, as they would centre on a breakdown of the pastoral relationship between incumbent and people. Otherwise the bishop would invite the complainant to complete a simple official complaint form. From that point the complaint would be an official disciplinary matter, and the bishop would follow the procedures outlined in Part B of this chapter.

(c)   If, at the other extreme, it is seen as a minor complaint of the kind that currently form the majority of the complaints made to a bishop, where formal disciplinary procedures are not warranted, then the bishop would follow the procedures for minor complaints outlined in Part A of this chapter. Here the emphasis is pastoral.

(d)   In between (b) and (c) above would come some cases where the gravity of the offence, if proven, would be less easy to define. In such cases, the minor complaints procedure (Part A) would be followed until and unless the seriousness of the case became more obvious. Only then would formal disciplinary procedures be followed.

We accept that, in a small number of instances, complainants would be unhappy with options (a), (c), or (d). Where this happens the bishop can invite the complainant to complete the simple official complaint form. Then, after further reflection, the bishop could follow route one under Part B, thereby concluding his part in the procedures.

Three questions about this way forward

WILL THESE PROPOSALS ENCOURAGE THE MAKING OF COMPLAINTS?

8.10   First, we must consider the context in which we live. In particular, three contemporary trends need to be recognised, for they affect the Church as much as they do society in general:

(a)   We live in a more litigious society than has been the case hitherto. This is a fact that needs to be faced, whether we welcome or whether we deplore it. People are more ready to have recourse to litigation, and we may expect this to happen in the Church, whether our disciplinary procedures are reformed or left untouched.

(b)   Allied to the more litigious nature of society, there is also a more ready recourse to devices like judicial review when people feel aggrieved or offended by decisions or procedures. We are aware that such recourse has been more openly considered in some quarters. It is not our place to comment on whether such action would be justified, wise, or helpful. But it is a reality that must be noted.

(c)   Ours is a society with a strong economic emphasis, and a desire for 'value for money'. The recent financial difficulties of the Church Commissioners have highlighted the cost of maintaining a stipendiary ministry. They have also left the Church of

England with a major challenge to become ever more financially self-sufficient. Many parishes will accept this challenge. But at the same time they may become much more interested in the quality of the minister whom they are now much more directly maintaining. What may have been tolerated in the past will no longer necessarily be countenanced in the future. Again, it is not the Working Party's task to pass comment upon the desirability of this trend. It is a fact to be faced, with very real implications in the area of discipline.

The three features of national and church life listed above suggest that the possibility of complaints being made is going to grow in the immediate future. That growth is likely whatever action we take or fail to take. What is more surprising is the relatively low level of complaints thus far. In part this is because the incidence of ecclesiastical offences is low in proportion to the numbers in Holy Orders. It is also due in part to the understandable reluctance hitherto for church members to make a complaint, even where this was justified.

8.11   We believe that the nature of the 1963 Measure discourages the making of complaints. A few have argued to us that this is a virtue in the present legislation; but we have remained unconvinced by this reasoning. We feel that to have a disciplinary procedure that makes complaining quite difficult is immoral. It is also counter-productive, for the one thing it will fail to achieve is a true reduction in complaints. All it will do is drive them underground, exacerbate frustrations, and lead to a range of responses that are less controllable, deny natural justice, and produce a series of ad hoc and highly inconsistent results.

8.12   So after careful weighing of the issues, and in the light of the context in which we live, we have concluded that what some might consider a freeing of the ability to lay a complaint is the best way forward. We wish to avoid obstacles that generate frustration or suspicion of those authorised to act. Equally, we wish to see complaints stated clearly and dealt with properly without undue delay. For alongside easier access to making a complaint must go appropriate measures to handle the complaint, and especially to reject it where it is found to be frivolous or malicious.

WILL THESE PROPOSALS MEAN MORE DISCIPLINARY CASES?

8.13   In so far as litigation is limited at present by the unwillingness of bishops (quite understandably) to employ the 1963 Measure, the answer must be in the affirmative. But it would be foolish to presume that discipline has only been proceeded with in three cases in 33 years. That is but the use of the ultimate procedure. The evidence is clear that it should have been used more often, but the Church has balked at the implications.

8.14   In each instance of a Consistory Court hearing there has been a hotly defended case, where the cleric concerned has protested his innocence of the charges laid against him. Our proposed Tribunal provides for the adjudications that contested cases should require. Shed of the disadvantages that lead people to avoid using the 1963 Measure's provision, it would be realistic to assume an increased use of the adjudicatory provision.

8.15   For 33 years most discipline has fallen into one of two broad categories:

● it has not been attempted. The problem simply endured until time has brought about a conclusion; or

● informal methods have been employed. Occasionally the Section 31 censure by consent provision has been used. More often, bearing in mind the frequency with which erring clerics acknowledge their guilt and do not wish to embarrass the Church, resignation by the cleric or revocation of licence (for those who do not have a freehold) have been the standard responses. While at times this has worked well, both for the cleric and the Church, it is in fact a perilous way forward without appropriate safeguards (see paragraph 8.50 below), and can often be misjudged.

WILL THESE PROPOSALS INCREASE THE BURDEN ON DIOCESAN BISHOPS?

8.16   It is our opinion that this should not happen.

(a)   Under the 1963 Measure the bishop is unable to act until a formal complaint is laid in the Diocesan Registry. He must then personally interview each complainant and the cleric involved. If the matter is to proceed further, it then goes out of his control. We have designed a new procedure in which (as we outlined in Chapter 4) the bishop is involved at an earlier stage and is to supervise the procedure. But this does not translate into a greater caseload. Indeed, it ought to be the reverse. Our understanding of the exercise of episcope is not of a bishop doing everything himself. Rather, he oversees the process, delegating most of the interviewing and investigating to others. His task is to 'hold the reins', and make the significant staging decisions on the basis of the advice he receives. We envisage the diocesan bishop delegating tasks, and making the final decisions in the light of the information with which he is provided.

(b)   We have also formulated our proposals in the light of what actually is happening, rather than on what the 1963 Measure presumed would happen. Consequently, our proposals encompass the range of complaints at present being handled, rather than extend the number. The caseload would only expand if the actual number of complaints, both serious and minor, both legitimate and frivolous, were to grow.

(c)   Our proposals, at all stages where the bishop is supervising the handling of a complaint, presume the use of existing resources. In addition to the diocesan staff (who are already involved at times) we suggest the use of rural deans, and suitable lay members. These resources already exist. The bishop is simply being encouraged to make use of his existing resources, and is given much wider freedom to respond to complaints in what he perceives to be the most appropriate way, Where, under our formal disciplinary procedures, a case goes to a hearing before the Tribunal, the resources are provided for at a national level, under the proposed new Measure.

Why introduce Codes of Practice?

8.17   The problem with legislation is that it takes a considerable time to enact. So in a Measure we want to provide a relevant simplified procedure for discipline, with sufficient flexibility to have enduring value.

Alongside the Measure (but required by it) there will be guidance to highlight best practice, and to define appropriate ways of carrying through the procedure. In the light of experience, such practices will need to be modified. Using a Measure this would be a lengthy and tortuous route. In Codes of Practice laid before the General Synod for approval by the Commission, those modifications can be made effectively and swiftly, without undue fuss, but in a responsible and accountable way.

8.18   The function of Codes of Practice, which should remain short and simple rather than become complex and confusing, is not to dictate style. They are there to warn against 'short cuts' in handling discipline, and to ensure a fair hearing. So often nowadays in law the substance of the issue is not addressed because the case is argued over technicalities and neglect for proper practice. Codes should guard against this and enable the substance of the complaint to be assessed and responded to.

8.19   Such Codes of Practice provide a framework of security for everyone concerned. The bishop or his agent is perceived to have investigated fairly, and not to be placing undue pressure on complainant or cleric. The cleric involved is assured of his right to defend himself with help. Precipitate action is avoided, and ongoing grievances should only surround the decision reached, not the procedure by which it was reached.

The new procedures in outline

8.20   Figure 8.1 shows the initial sieving or filtering procedure, which must be completed no more than four weeks after the complaint is received in writing by the bishop. In most instances, it will take much less than four weeks, and the bishop will proceed to (a), (b), (c), or (d) below well before the four week limit. The four weeks maximum is simply to prevent a case being stalled and delayed unreasonably.

8.21   Following the initial inquiry the bishop will, in the light of the information provided to him, take one of four courses of action:

(a)   dismiss the complaint as being frivolous or mischievous;

Figure 8.1   Initial procedure

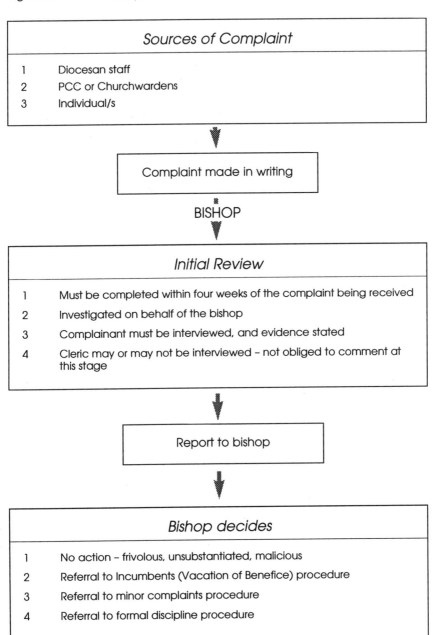

(b) direct it to be handled under the Incumbent (Vacation of Benefices) Measures of 1977 and 1993, if it concerns pastoral breakdown, etc.;

(c) continue with the minor complaints procedure in Part A below where it is a less serious complaint;

(d) invite the complainant to complete a simple complaint form, and proceed with formal disciplinary procedures where the allegation/s is serious.

Part A: Procedures for resolving minor complaints about the clergy

8.22 Minor complaints fall outside our remit. Nevertheless, clergy discipline forms part of a wider range of potential complaints and dissatisfactions. So this Part A is included to reflect that wider context, and to emphasise that only a limited range of complaints that are from time to time expressed to the bishop are relevant to the clergy discipline procedure.

8.23 We are grateful to the Clergy Conditions of Service Steering Group for their willingness to provide a suggested minor complaints procedure. This will be found at the end of our Report at Appendix C. It is entirely the work of the Steering Group, and we have no comment to make on it. It is offered for illustrative purposes, and, as it clearly indicates, would need to be revised after thorough consultation and discussion.

8.24 Our starting point is the wide range of possible complaints that a diocesan bishop might receive. As we have indicated already, a proper filtering process is needed. This would identify and eliminate the frivolous, the malicious and the inconsequential complaints. What should then be left is a number of quite legitimate complaints, most of which we believe will be fairly minor. As it would be in no one's interest to activate formal disciplinary procedures for fairly minor complaints, a simple procedure to handle these effectively is required. Borderline cases (see paragraph 8.9 (d) above) would be treated as minor unless or until their greater gravity became apparent. The intention is that formal discipline is only initiated when the alleged offence warrants such action.

8.25   We have recommended above that the initial filtering process should be completed in a period of no more than four weeks (see paragraph 8.8 above). Similarly we wish to see maximum time allowances given for the resolution of minor complaints, and for the stages of the formal disciplinary procedures. On occasion there may be genuine reasons to extend these time limits for discipline cases, and provision should be made for case direction orders to be made. But one of the serious criticisms of the 1963 Measure is the unduly lengthy nature of the procedures. Justice delayed is unhealthy. A new culture of avoiding delay is needed and should be written into the new Measure.

Part B: Formal disciplinary procedures

8.26   The procedures under the 1963 Measure require a trial to be conducted using the procedure of the Crown Court in a criminal trial. However, a criminal complaint would be investigated by the police and prosecuted by the Crown Prosecution Service. There are no equivalent organisations for dealing with complaints under the 1963 Measure. The result is that the gathering of evidence is somewhat haphazard and the conduct of prosecutions has to be undertaken on an ad hoc basis by private lawyers who may have had little or no practical experience of dealing with such matters and whose fees are therefore likely to reflect the novelty of the case. We have endeavoured in our recommendations to suggest ways in which both the investigation and the prosecution of complaints can be more efficiently dealt with by persons unconnected with the diocese where the complaint arises.

8.27   The procedure commences once the complainant has completed and returned the simple form. It is desirable that it should be clear to both the complainant and the bishop that the complaint is now to be treated as a formal complaint under the new procedure.

8.28   Once the formal complaint has been made to the bishop, there are four courses of action open to him (Figure 8.2 shows an overview of this procedure). He may decide:

Figure 8.2   Overview

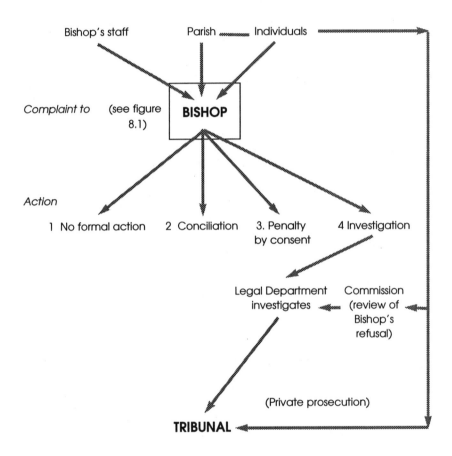

(a)   to take no formal action;

(b)   to refer the matter for conciliation;

(c)   to impose a penalty by consent;

(d)   that the complaint warrants further investigation with a view to prosecution, or that it is too serious a matter to be dealt with by (c) above and should go before the Tribunal.

These four options are considered in more detail below.

8.29   We recommend that the time-scales within which action must be taken should be prescribed by legislation or, in some cases, recommended in a Code of Practice. We see the production of a Code of Practice giving guidance on the way in which bishops should approach formal disciplinary complaints as an essential feature of the new system. We also recommend that the bishop should not, as he presently does, have a veto on the prosecution of complaints. If the bishop decides to take no formal action on a complaint received from a parish or an individual, we recommend that the complainant should have the right to a review of the bishop's decision by the Commission who may decide to refer the matter to the legal department. If the Commission declines to do so, there should be a residual right of private prosecution at the expense of the complainant. We also recommend that the rules of procedure for the Tribunal should enable the President to strike out a vexatious or malicious complaint at a preliminary hearing.

The new procedure in detail

8.30   We now look in detail at the four options open to the bishop following receipt of a formal written complaint.

No formal action (figure 8.3)

8.31   We suggest that complaints which do not justify further action may fall into one of two categories. Some complaints will be unfounded because they are malicious or mischievous or simply based on a misunderstanding. Other complaints may not justify formal action, but may

Figure 8.3   No formal action

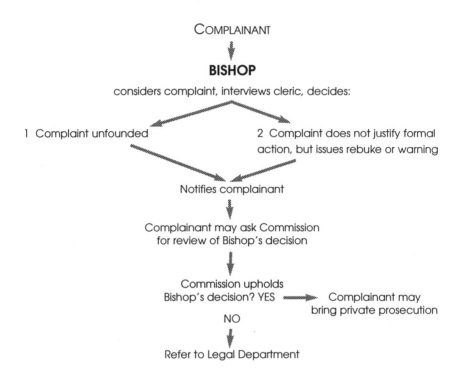

nevertheless suggest a misjudgement or departure from the expected standards by the cleric concerned. In the second category, the bishop may consider it appropriate to issue a rebuke or warning about the consequences of any repetition, or to put in place some system of monitoring or counselling. In either case, the bishop will notify the complainant in writing of his decision within a specified time from the complaint being made. If the complainant is dissatisfied he may ask the Commission to review the bishop's decision, and if the Commission declines to do so he may bring a private prosecution at his own expense.

CASE STUDY A : A VEXATIOUS COMPLAINT

Mrs Smith is an elderly widow living in a suburban parish. The vicar has a large and somewhat unruly family, several being in their early teens. One of the vicar's teenage sons has a pair of roller skates and frequently skates at some speed over the local pavements. On one occasion he almost knocks Mrs Smith over. She remonstrates with him and he calls her an interfering old bag. Mrs Smith is outraged and immediately writes to the bishop complaining that the vicar has failed (as he is required to do by Canon C 26) to be diligent to frame and fashion the life of his family according to the doctrines of Christ. The bishop writes back to Mrs Smith to the effect that there is always a balance to be drawn in controlling teenage children who are apt to be unruly, and that research has shown that if clergy children are subject to stricter discipline than is imposed in other families they may suffer psychological damage. Mrs Smith is not satisfied and demands that the bishop enforce the Canon. The bishop tells Mrs Smith that she may if she wishes make a formal complaint to him, and sends her a form for this purpose. Mrs Smith completes the form and sends it to the bishop.

The bishop telephones the vicar and suggests that he might try to encourage his children not to be offensive to parishioners. He then writes to Mrs Smith and says that he has determined to take no formal action on the complaint, but if she wishes she may ask the Clergy Discipline Commission to review his decision. Mrs Smith writes back to say that she is appalled at the bishop's willingness to tolerate a blatant breach of canon law and she is going to write to the Archbishop of Canterbury and the Queen. The bishop responds to the effect that he has dealt with the matter in accordance with the law and his role is now at an end. He reminds Mrs Smith of her remedy if she is dissatisfied.

Mrs Smith applies to the Clergy Discipline Commission to review the bishop's decision. The Commission, with little hesitation, supports the bishop's decision and refuses to refer the matter to the Legal Department. The Secretary to the Commission advises Mrs Smith that she may if she wishes pursue a private prosecution before the Clergy Discipline Tribunal.

Mrs Smith issues proceedings in the Tribunal. The proceedings are served on the vicar whose response to the Tribunal is that the complaint is frivolous and vexatious and an abuse of the process of the Tribunal. The matter is referred to the President of the Tribunal who, after giving Mrs Smith the opportunity to make representations to him, strikes out the complaint as being frivolous and vexatious and orders that Mrs Smith pay the costs.

Figure 8.4   Conciliation

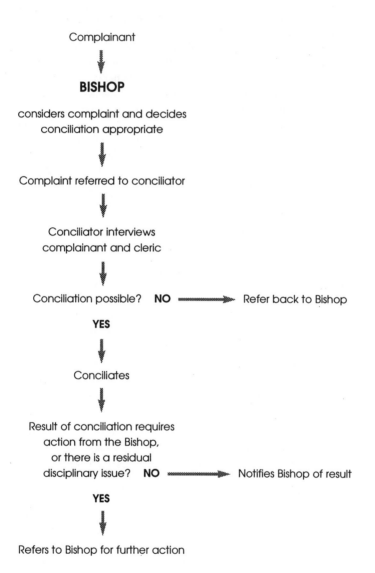

Complainant

BISHOP

considers complaint and decides
conciliation appropriate

Complaint referred to conciliator

Conciliator interviews
complainant and cleric

Conciliation possible?   **NO** ⟶ Refer back to Bishop

YES

Conciliates

Result of conciliation requires
action from the Bishop,
or there is a residual
disciplinary issue?   **NO** ⟶ Notifies Bishop of result

YES

Refers to Bishop for further action

CONCILIATION (FIGURE 8.4)

8.32   It has been submitted to us that conciliation or mediation should be attempted in all discipline cases. We disagree. We believe that this submission is based on a mistaken premise that all discipline cases are in the nature of a dispute between a cleric and the bishop or a third party which is susceptible of resolution by conciliation. Whilst there will be some cases where conciliation would be appropriate, there will be others where the alleged offence amounts to an offence against the Church generally and where, if the offence is proved, a penalty should be imposed. We also believe that there are cases where there is a place for both conciliation and discipline. It may be possible to resolve the grievance of a particular parishioner, but that grievance may arise from the commission of an offence by the cleric which should be dealt with. We therefore recommend that conciliation should be available in appropriate cases but it should not be a mandatory route for all cases, nor should it necessarily represent the entirety of the disciplinary process.

8.33   If the bishop receives a written complaint and considers that conciliation may be appropriate, and the complainant and cleric are both willing for the matter to be conciliated (a prerequisite of any conciliation), the bishop may refer the matter to a conciliator. We have it in mind that bishops, perhaps with guidance from the Commission, would have a number of people in the diocese available to be called upon to fulfil the role of conciliator.

8.34   If the conciliator is unable to achieve conciliation within a specified time (which could be extended by the consent of both parties) the matter would be referred back to the bishop who would then have to choose one of the other three courses of action open to him. If conciliation is possible, the conciliator would report back to the bishop with the result of the conciliation. As we have said, there may be a residual disciplinary complaint (for example, an individual's complaint is resolved to his satisfaction, but the cleric's attitude generally suggests a failure to comply with the Canons). The bishop would then decide what further action, if any, was appropriate. It is also possible that the result of the conciliation may require further, non-disciplinary action from the bishop.

81

CASE STUDY B : A MORE DIFFICULT COMPLAINT

The benefice is vacant. The benefice comprises a single parish which has a parish church and a daughter church. For many years the parish church has used ASB Rite A Holy Communion. The daughter church, which has a much smaller congregation, has been accustomed to The Book of Common Prayer.

A new vicar is appointed. She indicates to the Parochial Church Council her wish to use Rite A in the daughter church as well and the PCC is split, but a motion to agree to the use of Rite A in the daughter church is lost by one vote. The vicar announces that she intends, in any event, on an experimental basis to use Rite A in the daughter church. She points out that the majority of the worshipping community in the parish are accustomed to Rite A. She also refers to Article XXIV in the 39 Articles and says that in her opinion The Book of Common Prayer is written in a tongue not understanded of the people. At the next service of Holy Communion at the daughter church the vicar uses Rite A.

A complaint is made to the bishop by the worshippers at the daughter church that the vicar is in breach of Canon B 3 and should not have changed the form of service without the consent of the Parochial Church Council. The bishop ascertains that this is a formal complaint and considers that it may be suitable for conciliation. The complainants and the vicar agree to conciliation and the bishop appoints a conciliator.

There are two possible endings.

Ending 1

Through the actions of the conciliator, the parish and the incumbent agree that ASB Rite B will be used on an experimental basis. The matter is resolved to everyone's satisfaction. The bishop suggests to the vicar that in future she should observe the requirements of Canon B 3, but there are no residual disciplinary issues and so the complaint has been dealt with.

Ending 2

The conciliator is unable to secure an agreement between the vicar and the complainants and refers the matter back to the bishop. The bishop points out to the vicar that canon law is on the side of the parishioners and asks her to revert to the use of The Book of Common Prayer until the PCC agrees to a change. The vicar refuses and says that she intends to use Rite A irrespective of the Canons. The bishop therefore refers the matter to the Legal Department for investigation and possible prosecution before the Clergy Discipline Tribunal.

Figure 8.5   Penalty by consent

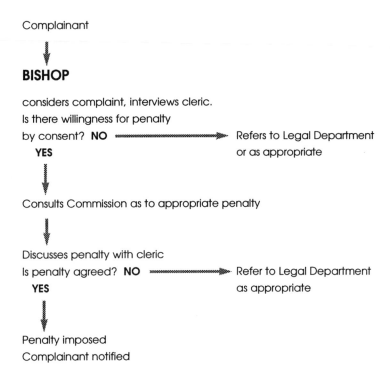

Complainant

BISHOP

considers complaint, interviews cleric.
Is there willingness for penalty
by consent? **NO** ━━━━━━━━━━▶ Refers to Legal Department
　　YES　　　　　　　　　　　　　or as appropriate

Consults Commission as to appropriate penalty

Discusses penalty with cleric
Is penalty agreed? **NO** ━━━━━━━━▶ Refer to Legal Department
　　YES　　　　　　　　　　　　　as appropriate

Penalty imposed
Complainant notified

PENALTY BY CONSENT (FIGURE 8.5)

8.35   Under the 1963 Measure the bishop may impose censure by consent if a formal complaint has been laid before the Consistory Court. We advocate retention of the possibility of disposing of complaints through the imposition of a penalty by consent, but in a different form.

8.36   The 1963 Measure appears to envisage that a cleric will agree to the imposition of censure by consent in general and it will then be for the bishop to decide on the appropriate penalty to impose. We had assumed that, in reality, a cleric would not consent to a penalty without knowing what the penalty was going to be. However, we have received anecdotal evidence that this is not the case, and that clerics consent to censure assuming they will receive perhaps a rebuke or monition only to discover that the bishop has decided on deprivation. We do not believe that this is satisfactory. We recommend that there should be consent both as to the imposition of a penalty and as to the penalty to be imposed, and we believe that there should, in the Code of Practice, be safeguards to ensure that clerics (who are perhaps in a state of shock or discomposure because of events which have occurred or been made public) have the chance to reflect on the proposed penalty and to take independent advice before giving their consent.

8.37   We therefore recommend that where a complaint is made to the bishop and the cleric accepts the imposition of a penalty, the bishop should consider what the appropriate penalty should be given the facts which have been admitted. We envisage that the Clergy Discipline Commission would issue appropriate guidelines to help bishops in this respect. The bishop will then formulate his views as to the penalty which should be imposed and will discuss this with the cleric concerned. If the cleric is not prepared to accept the penalty then the bishop will take one of the other courses of action open to him on receipt of a complaint, and in most cases this will mean a reference to the legal department. If there is agreement as to the penalty, it can be imposed and the complainant notified. The penalty should then be recorded, perhaps by both Provincial Registrars as well as the Registrar of the Tribunal. Following the imposition of a penalty by consent there could be no further proceedings against the cleric arising from the admitted facts.

8.38   We have considered two subsidiary issues. First, the complainant may be dissatisfied with the penalty imposed, particularly if the bishop has imposed a more lenient penalty than that recommended by the Commission. Should the complainant be able to take any further action in this situation? We believe not. It would be wrong for the cleric to face the risk of double jeopardy and reliance must be placed on the wisdom and judgement of the bishop having consulted with the Commission. Secondly, under the present procedure there may be censure by consent at any stage in the proceedings, thereby bringing the proceedings to an end. Should this be preserved even where proceedings have been issued in the Tribunal? Again we believe not. We suggest that once a complaint has been referred to the Tribunal, the complaint should be in the hands of the Tribunal alone to deal with.

CASE STUDY C: A CLEAR CASE

From the very commencement of his ministry in the parish, the vicar's strongly held views on Third World matters were evident. A significant part of his time was given to relief agency work and to making political representations. Following complaints from dissatisfied parishioners, the bishop had twice defended his right to express his political views, but advised him to give more of his time to his parochial responsibilities.

Following a change of PCC treasurer, the payment of the parochial quota to the diocese became increasingly intermittent, and, eventually, it ceased to be paid. The archdeacon visited the parish to find out why it was not being paid, and discovered that the new treasurer was having difficulty in balancing the accounts. Upon further enquiry, unauthorised sums amounting to some £12,000 were found to have been removed from the parish's general account and fabric fund over a period of four years. These had all been amounts required by the vicar, which the retired treasurer had forwarded to the vicar upon his demand. Some had gone as donations to relief agency crisis appeals; one was to fund legal representations by the vicar on behalf of an illegal immigrant; several conferences attended by the vicar had been paid for in this way; and the biggest amount was to finance the vicar's three month sabbatical study tour of Africa and Asia.

Eventually the archdeacon felt obliged to lay a formal complaint before the bishop, who asked to see the vicar. Upon outlining the nature of the complaint and emphasising its seriousness . . . . .

Ending 1

. . . . . the vicar admitted the offences, the seriousness of which he had failed to perceive. He accepted the need for discipline and placed himself voluntarily under the bishop's censure. After reviewing the situation with the churchwardens and the PCC, the bishop issued both a conditional discharge for five years and an injunction preventing the vicar from being a signatory for cheques drawn on PCC accounts.

Ending 2

. . . . . the vicar contested the seriousness of the allegations. He maintained that the monies were properly spent as an extension of his parochial ministry, and that Third World needs were a far more urgent and appropriate demand than propping up the diocesan finances. As the vicar denied the charges of financial mismanagement, the bishop passed the matter to the Commission. The ensuing Tribunal found the allegations proved. They ordered his removal from office and disqualified him for a five-year period.

Figure 8.6   Investigation

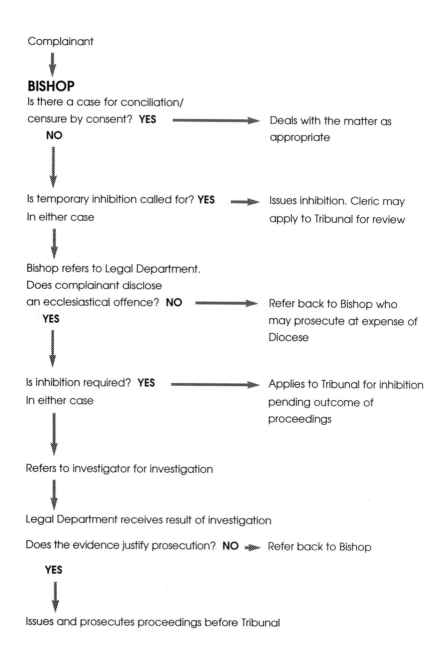

Complainant

BISHOP
Is there a case for conciliation/
censure by consent? **YES** ⟹ Deals with the matter as
    NO   appropriate

Is temporary inhibition called for? **YES** ⟹ Issues inhibition. Cleric may
In either case   apply to Tribunal for review

Bishop refers to Legal Department.
Does complainant disclose
an ecclesiastical offence? **NO** ⟹ Refer back to Bishop who
    YES   may prosecute at expense of
                                                          Diocese

Is inhibition required? **YES** ⟹ Applies to Tribunal for inhibition
In either case   pending outcome of
                                                        proceedings

Refers to investigator for investigation

Legal Department receives result of investigation

Does the evidence justify prosecution? **NO** ⟹ Refer back to Bishop

    YES

Issues and prosecutes proceedings before Tribunal

However, if the accused cleric does not dispute the allegation and, in effect, pleads guilty, the Tribunal should be able to deal with the imposition of a penalty in a private hearing without a full trial.

INVESTIGATION AND PROSECUTION (FIGURE 8.6)

8.39   This is the procedure which would apply where the bishop, having received a complaint, considers that it does warrant formal action and neither conciliation nor penalty by consent is appropriate.

8.40   In these cases the bishop would refer the complaint to the legal department who would consider the complaint and decide whether, as a matter of law, the allegations made disclosed an ecclesiastical offence. If the legal department took the view that they did not, they would refer the matter back to the bishop who would have the option (if he did not accept the legal department's decision) of prosecuting the case at the diocese's expense. If an offence was disclosed, the legal department would refer the case to an investigator for investigation.   Having received the result of the investigation the legal department would decide whether the evidence justified prosecution.

8.41   As stated above, we recommend that the standard of proof should continue to be proof beyond all reasonable doubt, and a judgement would therefore need to be formed as to whether the evidence would 'stand up in court' with a reasonable prospect of the complaint being proved, and also whether the allegation as supported by the evidence was sufficiently serious to warrant a prosecution. If the answers to these questions were in the negative, the legal department would refer the matter back to the bishop who again would have the right to prosecute at the expense of the diocese. If the answers were in the affirmative, the legal department would issue proceedings before the Tribunal and conduct the prosecution.

CASE STUDY D : A COMPLICATED CASE

The bishop receives a stongly worded complaint. A husband alleges that, during several pre-Baptism visits to his wife, the vicar was overly familiar. The bishop contacts the local rural dean, asking him to visit the complainant, and quietly to calm the situation.

The rural dean reports back that he has been unable to defuse the situation. Upon inquiry, the vicar has a reputation for flamboyance, and for being something of a 'ladies man'. There are a number of rumours in the parish, and the rural dean is led to believe that a further complaint is on the way to he bishop.

The bishop contacts the vicar and asks to see him. By the time of the interview the bishop has received two further complaints; one of sexual harrassment, and one of seduction. The bishop outlines these complaints to the vicar.

There are at least three possible responses:

1.   The vicar admits the seduction, and offers his resignation.

2.   The vicar accepts some carelessness on his part, but offers an alternative explanation of the alleged events.

3.   The vicar vehemently denies the allegations, and indicates his intention of suing the complainants for defamation.

In all three cases the bishop insists on a week for both of them to consider the situation. He strongly urges the vicar to seek advice, and indicates the potential seriousness of at least two of the allegations. He suggests that the vicar may wish to be accompanied by a friend/union rep/lawyer when they next meet. In responses 1 and 2 the vicar agrees to the bishop's suggestion to withdraw from ministry for the next week. In response 3 the bishop formally suspends the vicar for a week, as he is unwilling to withdraw voluntarily.

By the time they meet again, a further complaint has been made to the bishop of a long-term adulterous relationship with one of the Sunday School teachers.

The meeting is a formal interview. The vicar is accompanied by his union rep, and the bishop has his registrar in attendance. There are several possible endings:

Ending 1

The vicar is racked with guilt and offers to resign his living. The bishop is happy to allow this, but considers that this is insufficient to signal the church's disapproval of the vicar's conduct and to protect other parishes from a repetition of it. He therefore indicates that if the matter is to be dealt with by him it must be on the basis of the imposition of a penalty by consent. The vicar agrees to this.

Ending 2

The vicar admits the adulterous affair, but denies the seduction, and contests the other two allegations. After further inquiry the bishop decides that the sexual harrassment charge is without substance. It is dismissed as a malicious allegation, based upon anger at the vicar's quite correct refusal to permit a photograph of the deceased on a proposed funeral memorial. The situation proceds ultimately on the one charge, as in Ending 1.

Ending 3

The vicar denies the charges/seeks to justify them/is advised to resist them. So the bishop refers the matter to the Legal Department.

The matter is then out of the bishop's hands. The Legal Department confirms that, if proven, the allegations constitute offences under ecclesiastical law. They arrange for the investigator to gather the evidence. As a result, the baptism visit allegation is dropped as the evidence is considered inadequate and questionable. The alleged seduction is left on the file as the principal witness, whilst adamant about the facts, is unprepared to stand as a witness. In the case of the adulterous relationship allegation, the evidence does stand up, and so the Legal Department issues proceedings in the Tribunal, and applies for the suspension to be continued pending a hearing by the Tribunal. The Tribunal hears the case and finds it proved. It orders that the vicar be removed from office and prohibited indefinitely from exercising his orders

The use of suspension pending investigation and/or adjudication

8.42   The subsidiary issue of inhibition *pendente lite* arises here. This is the power at present contained in section 77 of the 1963 Measure which arises once proceedings under the Measure for an ecclesiastical offence or proceedings in the temporal courts for a criminal offence are pending. The bishop is able to inhibit the cleric from performing any services of the Church within his diocese until the proceedings are concluded. We recommend that this power should be retained, but in an enhanced form. We also recommend that it should be referred to as suspension rather than inhibition.

8.43   Allegations may come to the bishop which are so serious that the bishop considers that the cleric should immediately be suspended from exercising his office whilst the complaint is being investigated. We recommend that the bishop be given the power to impose a suspension where a complaint is made to him, but that the cleric should have the right to apply to the Tribunal for a review of the suspension. We also recommend that subject to any review by the Tribunal, the suspension should remain in force for a specified period of time or until proceedings are issued before the Tribunal, unless the suspension is renewed by the Tribunal. We have in mind a fairly short maximum period, perhaps one month. If this did not allow sufficient time for the conclusion of the investigation or if the investigation was in abeyance pending the outcome of secular criminal proceedings, the legal department would have to apply to the Tribunal for the suspension to be extended. Similarly, if proceedings were issued in the Tribunal, an interlocutory application for the suspension to be continued pending the outcome of the proceedings would have to be made.

8.44   We believe that in many cases, the existence of the power to suspend would result in a voluntary undertaking being given by the cleric, thereby avoiding the need for the issue of a formal suspension.

Complaints against bishops

8.45   We believe that essentially the same procedure (though with necessary modifications) should be applied whether the accused is a deacon, priest or bishop (including archbishops). We do not believe that there is any justification for retaining a procedure for the trial of bishops which is so cumbersome that it will never be used. We therefore propose that the Tribunal should be able to hear cases against clergy of all degrees. We believe that what is just and equitable for priests and deacons should be just and equitable for bishops too. We do, however, recommend that the membership of the Tribunal when constituted to try a bishop should include, as the clerical member, a person in episcopal orders.

Complaints against deans, provosts, archdeacons and residentiary canons

8.46   As with bishops, we consider that the same procedure should be used where the accused is a dean, provost, archdeacon or residentiary canon. We do not see the need for the clerical member of the Tribunal to hold an office similar to that of the accused. We note that the Archbishops' Commission on Cathedrals (*Heritage and Renewal*, 1994) proposed that a tribunal should be established to deal with the problem of 'ineffective' cathedral clergy (Chapter 8, paragraph 30). We would not favour the establishment of another tribunal and would recommend that the Incumbents (Vacation of Benefices) Measures 1977 and 1993 be modified to take account of infirm cathedral clergy and archdeacons and be extended to cover ineffective clergy holding any office.

Appeals

8.47   We recommend that appeals from the Tribunal should in all cases go to the Court of Arches or the Chancery Court of York and be heard by the Dean of Arches/Auditor sitting with two Tribunal chairmen who were not involved in the original hearing.

8.48   We recommend that there should be an appeal as of right against the penalty imposed, and with the leave of the Tribunal or the appellate court, on a point of law, or where it is alleged that the decision was one which no reasonable Tribunal would have reached. We also recommend that there should be a right to apply to the appellate court to order a re-hearing if new evidence comes to light which might have influenced the result of the original trial had it been available at the time.

Censure by consent

8.49   In principle, there is nothing wrong with this resolution of disciplinary matters. Often it will open the way to ongoing service in an appropriate capacity without undue damage to the cleric, the Church, or the bishop. In a society where media exposure can sometimes be exaggerated or intense, this is often to be welcomed. Our third option (paragraphs 8.35 to 8.38) preserves the possibility of censure by consent, and we hope that it will become a more well-used option. The only limitation we have added is for the bishop to consult with the Commission over which penalties would be appropriate, and for his final decision to be agreed with the cleric concerned. In this way some reasonable consistency should be achieved in the penalties imposed, thereby eradicating an existing area of grievance, without extinguishing a reasonable discretion for the bishop. Equally, if the proposed penalty is clearly stated and accepted by the cleric, there will be no sense of injustice resulting from misunderstanding or a late change of mind by the bishop.

Volunteering to resign

8.50   In a significant number of cases the erring cleric concedes the allegation, and offers to resign. More often than not a bishop accepts such an offer. But we believe that care needs to be exercised, on a number of grounds:

(a)   Some clergy can be naive and easily swayed, especially where they harbour a sense of guilt for the way in which they have fallen short. In such a situation resignation may be the obvious but inappropriate way out. Or it may be difficult to resist the suggestion to 'do the decent thing' by resigning. For:

- the offence may not be serious enough to warrant loss of job

- resignation may allow the cleric to avoid facing the gravity of the offence

- resignation may prevent the Church from stating its displeasure, or from recording the disciplinary offence.

(b)   It is not only the cleric who is involved. Often there is a congregation and a parish to be considered. For many clergy there are a spouse and children involved. Resignation normally means loss of income and also of accommodation. Both parish and family are intimately affected, and need to be included in the equation. At the very least, the spouse and the churchwardens need to be consulted and made aware of the options.

(c) There is also the complainant, and/or the victims of indiscretions, to be considered. A swift and ill-considered resignation may well be viewed more negatively by them than by the bishop.

8.51 We would suggest that, where an offer to resign is made, there should be a seven-day period for all parties to reflect upon the proposal.

(a) This would give the bishop time (especially when the situation has been sprung on him at little or no notice) to consider whether a resignation is appropriate in the circumstances. It would also permit him time to seek legal advice and, we would suggest, to receive an objective second opinion.

(b) Where an offer to resign has been made out of an initial sense of honour, because of a feeling of guilt, under duress, or as a gut reaction without much thought, the seven-day period would allow time to review that response, and to seek advice, before it becomes irrevocable.

If, after seven days, both parties agree to a resignation, then it proceeds with it being clearly understood that it will be recorded on the Caution List as a resignation made in disciplinary circumstances.

8.52 In the case of a Deed of Relinquishment being signed, or of a penalty being applied, the position is recorded (rightly) on the Caution List. In such cases the guilty cleric is at present debarred from being admitted to a new office, or, if the cleric is not debarred, his or her disciplinary record is available when an appointment is being considered.

8.53 At present, a resignation conveniently ignores all this, and leaves the way open to a new appointment. This is unfair and needs to be corrected. The simplest answer is for Part 1 of the Caution List to include all Deeds of Relinquishment, Disqualifications and Prohibitions. Part 2, where a new appointment is possible, would record all other penalties and cases of resignation in disciplinary cases.

9

ECCLESIASTICAL
DISCIPLINARY PENALTIES

9.1   We have suggested in previous chapters that it is entirely proper for those in Holy Orders to come under an understood standard of discipline. Not only is this helpful to the individual cleric, in clarifying what is to be expected; it is also an assurance to the Church and to our society. Clergy are to live by certain standards, and, if they fall short of these, they should be open to investigation and held to account.

9.2   But no system of discipline will carry weight unless, in addition to upholding expected standards and investigating where it is alleged that these have been breached, there is some facility for taking appropriate action. Under the 1963 Measure the responses that can be made to breaches of clerical discipline are called 'censures'. Their existence emphasises how seriously breaches of the discipline will be viewed, and assures everyone that action can and will be taken when clergy fall short.

9.3   The 1963 Measure (section 49) provides five 'Censures' to which clergy may be liable if found guilty of an offence under that Measure. They are:

- deprivation (and, sometimes, deposition)
- inhibition
- suspension
- monition
- rebuke

In fact, only two of these censures have ever been imposed by a Consistory Court: deprivation (Tyler) and rebuke (Bland, whose original censure of deprivation was reduced on appeal to a rebuke). It is also possible for these censures to be applied by the bishop where, under section 31 of the 1963 Measure, a cleric admits guilt and surrenders voluntarily to censure by the bishop. Where a cleric has been involved in certain proceedings of the secular courts, under section 55 of the Measure, deprivation is automatic without any further trial by the Church, and deposition may follow. Currently only the Reverend Thomas Tyler will appear on Part 1 of the Archbishops' Caution List as a result of a Consistory Court Judgement. Other names in that part of the List will be the result of section 31 (sentence by consent) proceedings or section 55 (secular court) proceedings. Our understanding is that the only penalties involved are those of deprivation and deposition.

9.4   So, in 33 years, little or no use has been made of inhibition, suspension, or monition. This alone suggests that the existing provision of censures is in need of review.

9.5   We were agreed that the language used to describe the existing censures under section 49 of the Measure is somewhat obscure. In our review we have been concerned to:

- examine the practical use of the existing censures;

- ensure that adequate powers are made available to the Tribunal and to the bishops;

- modernise the terminology employed in a future Measure.

In achieving these goals it is perhaps a useful starting point to consider in some detail the existing censures.

The existing censures

(1)   DEPRIVATION

This involves removal from any preferment held by the cleric. It also means that no further preferment is possible, save under certain specified circumstances. So this censure includes both deprivation and disqualification, from freehold office and any office to which a cleric can be licensed. But it imposes no bar on holding permission to officiate.

9.7   Subject to proper notice being given, and to the cleric concerned having a one-month period in which to appeal to the archbishop, the diocesan bishop, upon a censure of deprivation being given, may proceed without any further legal proceedings, to depose the cleric ('de-frocking' in common parlance).

9.8   A disqualified cleric may be given preferment in the future with the consent of the archbishop and the bishop of the diocese in which the proceedings originated. When this happens the archbishop may direct that the disqualification ceases. Alternatively, the disqualification could remain for any subsequent appointment, thereby creating, in effect, a trial appointment. One question that requires answering is whether it is appropriate that the sentence of the court can be overridden in this way, or whether the removal or variation of the disqualification should be a matter for the Tribunal.

(2)   INHIBITION

9.9   This is disqualification for a specified period of time from exercising any of the functions of Holy Orders. Inhibition, therefore, prevents the disciplined cleric from acting as a priest in any capacity, as not even permission to officiate is possible. To that extent it is a more severe censure than is the disqualification in (1) above. But it is for a limited period of time, presumably because an indefinite inhibition would be tantamount to deposition from Holy Orders.

(3)   SUSPENSION

9.10   This is disqualification for a specified time from exercising or performing any right or duty incidental to the cleric's preferment, or from residing in the house of residence of the preferment, or within a specified distance of the house of residence, without leave of the bishop. We need to consider whether there are, in reality, any circumstances where suspension is likely to be imposed as a disciplinary censure rather than as a temporary measure pending the determination of a complaint.

9.11   Would it really be practicable for an incumbent or curate to be suspended for, say, six or twelve months? Presumably, if a stipendiary, he would still be paid. But somebody else would have to be appointed to perform the duties which he was suspended from performing, with relevant financial provision. Nor would it be realistic to prevent a cleric from residing in the parsonage or curacy house for the specified period of time. Where else would he and his family reside, and what would happen to all their furniture and possessions? We would, therefore, suggest that suspension be excluded as a disciplinary censure.

9.12   In passing we note the 'sting in the tail' introduced by section 49(2) of the 1963 Measure. In the case of inhibitions and suspensions, where a censure has been pronounced, the cleric cannot be readmitted to his preferment, nor be allowed to exercise the functions of Holy Orders, unless he satisfies the bishop of his good conduct during the suspension or inhibition. Apart from the denial of natural justice involved in there being no right of appeal if the bishop declares himself to be dissatisfied, there is also very real vagueness around what is meant by '*good conduct*'. If the cleric has been censured for an offence concerning the way in which the clerical duties were performed, how can subsequent good conduct be established when the cleric is debarred from performance of his duties? Or is the intention that the cleric can satisfy the bishop as to his good conduct in a more general way, such as by undertaking voluntary work? However wise the underlying intention of section 49(2) might have been, the out-working is too vague, and a hostage to arbitrary decision.

(4)   MONITION

This is a direction to do something, or an order to refrain from doing something. For a first offence involving doctrine, ritual or ceremonial, monition is the most severe penalty that can be imposed at present. In some form this would be an eminently suitable censure. But at present, beyond further prosecution for a repeated offence, there is no means of enforcement.

9.14   Especially in the case of a doctrinal offence we would need to question the usefulness of monition. Where an illegal form of service is the problem, a monition might be entirely appropriate. Likewise, if a cleric were preaching some fairly new and radical doctrines he might not realise that they were heretical until found guilty by the Court, and so monition would be an appropriate initial censure. However, there could be serious doctrinal cases where monition would be somewhat ridiculous. A cleric who preaches the belief that God does not exist should cease to be a cleric (if, in conscience, he has not already resigned his Holy Orders). But as the law stands all he can receive is a monition. Presumably, this would require him either to start believing in God, or to stop telling his parishioners that he did not believe in God!

(5)   REBUKE

9.15   This speaks for itself and should probably be retained. However, a prosecution that leads only to a rebuke would probably be a prosecution which should not have been brought. As will be seen from the minor complaints procedures outlined in Appendix C, rebuke will be a penalty available in those circumstances.

Proposed new penalties

9.16   As with other parts of the disciplinary system in the 1963 Measure we concluded that consideration of appropriate penalties should start afresh. Furthermore, we recommend that the word 'censures' be replaced with the more readily understood word 'penalties'. We would recommend that the following penalties should be available, where a cleric is found guilty of an ecclesiastical offence:

(1)   REMOVAL FROM OFFICE

This would replace the present deprivation, and revocation of licence for disciplinary matters. It would mean the loss of current preferment, and nothing more.

Removal could be a sufficient penalty in its own right, allowing the cleric to seek an alternative office (e.g., a cleric who inadequately met the challenges of his current posting might be found better suited postings elsewhere). However, in the more serious cases, removal would be combined with either (2) or (3) below.

(2)   DISQUALIFICATION

This could be a penalty in its own right where imposed upon a cleric who holds no office. It could also be an additional penalty to removal from office ((1) above).

Where a cleric has been making a bad job of the office which he holds, but might be perfectly well suited to a different job in a different place, then removal from office is sufficient, and disqualification inappropriate. By way of contrast, however, when a cleric is found guilty of behaviour incompatible with his Orders, then disqualification needs to be considered in addition to his being removed from office. This would prevent appointment to a new office.

After a given period of time (say three years) it should be possible for the cleric to request that the disqualification be lifted, and for the Tribunal to consider this.   If the request is not granted, the cleric should be free to reapply at clearly stated intervals (maybe of one or two years).

(3)   PROHIBITION

Under this penalty the cleric would be prohibited from exercising his orders in any way at all, either for a specified period, or indefinitely. Where the prohibition is for an indefinite period, then the bishop may proceed to deposition, either on the advice of the Tribunal, or directly on his own assessment of the gravity of the offence.

Like disqualification, the censure of prohibition should be available on its own where a cleric holds no office, or combined with removal from office. Where the prohibition is indefinite, but does not lead to deposition, then, like disqualification, there should be a right to request the lifting of the prohibition after a specified period of time (say five years, as this is a censure for the most serious offences).

(4)   INJUNCTION

This would be a monition, but with teeth. The cleric could be restrained from doing a specified act, or required to do a specified act, by injunction, with the prospect of contempt of court if the injunction is not obeyed. In principle this is straightforward. In practice, it is more likely to be useful to restrain than to require. A cleric found guilty of financial irregularities might be restrained from handling the church collections. But it would be more problematic to require a cleric to be more diligent in sick visiting, or to baptise a baby of whose parents he did not approve.

This proposed censure might also be helpful in handling those who, under the guise of permission to officiate, become effectively 'free agents', taking little or no notice of their own bishop's instructions, or of diocesan boundaries. It might be possible to injunct such a cleric only to serve in a specified area, or to injunct him not to take worship in buildings licensed by the Church of England. Disregard of such an injunction would be a contempt of court.

(5)   CONDITIONAL DISCHARGE

It might be valuable to have a penalty to replace monition in less serious cases where an injunction would be inappropriate or unnecessarily heavy-handed. For example, a cleric who used an illegal form of service could be conditionally discharged for a specified period (say two years), a condition being that he did not continue to use the illegal form of service. Then, if he broke the condition he would be liable to receive a penalty for the original offence.

(6)   DEFERRED SENTENCE

In paragraph 8.12 we expressed concern about section 49(2) of the present 1963 Measure. What that section is presumably seeking to achieve might be better provided for by giving a power to defer sentence for six months or more, and then to determine the penalty in the light of the cleric's behaviour during that period.

(7)   REBUKE

This should continue to be available. Alternatively, written advice might be given, if a rebuke is felt to be too heavy.

(8)   ABSOLUTE DISCHARGE

This might be appropriate where, technically, an ecclesiastical offence has occurred, but where even a rebuke might be unnecessary. It acknowledges the offence without incurring any ongoing penalty.

9.17   All penalties, whether given by the Tribunal, or by the bishop giving censure by consent (see Chapter 8, paragraphs 35 to 38), should be recorded on the Caution List, in what is currently Part 1. This should be automatic, since it is no more than a statement of fact (see below in paragraph 9.22).

9.18   When giving censure by consent (see paragraphs 8.35 to 8.38) the bishop should be free to impose whichever penalty he considers appropriate, save that:

- if he considers **prohibition** to be appropriate, he must refer that to the Tribunal to be ratified. This is necessary as, once an indefinite prohibition is given the bishop may proceed, without further legal proceedings, to deposition. It would be unwise for a bishop to do this, however justified he considered the case, without confirmation by another party;

- if he considers an **injunction** to be appropriate, he must refer that to the Tribunal. As contempt of court is the consequence of disregard for an injunction, it is important that a legally constituted tribunal issues the injunction.

In both these cases, censure by consent can occur only where guilt is admitted. So the Tribunal is not called upon to adjudicate the facts of the case, but only the penalties, on the bishop's recommendation. It also provides appeal against the proposed penalty if the erring cleric considers it to be unreasonable.

Other issues

CROWN APPOINTMENTS

9.19   Under section 49(4) of the 1963 Measure, the Crown must confirm a deprivation censure for any person holding a non-parochial preferment where the right to appoint is vested in Her Majesty. Obviously, we would wish to consult before framing the new legislation. But we perceive real problems if the Tribunal were to censure by prohibition, but the Crown vetoed the removal from office of a bishop or a dean. Whilst we think this to be most unlikely, we need to ensure full consultation when the new Measure is drafted, so that the Crown as well as the Church has confidence in the new system of ecclesiastical discipline.

ROYAL PARDON

9.20   Section 53 of the 1963 Measure allows for the exercise of the Royal Pardon. Given that the Ecclesiastical Courts are the Queen's Courts this provision should be retained. It could be useful in cases where there would otherwise be an injustice for which the system provided no adequate redress.

APPEALS

9.21   The disciplinary procedures that we are recommending in Chapter 8 have a variety of appeal options written in. It would seem to us right that there should be the possibility of appeal over the penalty imposed. In the case of censure by consent we presume that the cleric will clarify the proposed penalty before he voluntarily submits to his bishop. So appeals here should be few, and the cleric may be required to explain why he now appeals when he previously submitted. However, we must allow for misunderstandings and confusions, and for bishops who change their mind at the last minute.

EXPUNGING OF THE RECORD

9.22   Once a censure has been served, the question arises as to how long, if at all, a record of the offence is to remain. In some instances we can see that the exhausting of the penalty should complete the episode. In other cases it would be important for an ongoing record to be kept.

We would suggest, therefore, that the Caution List consist of at least four parts:

Part 1 – all depositions, deeds of relinquishment and cases where the currently operational penalty debars a cleric from ordained ministry or admission to a clerical office;

Part 2 – all other penalties not yet spent;

Part 3 – all exhausted penalties. In the case of criminal offences adjudicated in the secular courts, a penalty shall remain on the record for as long as it would remain in the secular realm under the Rehabilitation of Offenders Act. Where the discipline was internal to the Church, it should remain for a minimum period of five or ten years (as specified by the Tribunal at the time of sentence); and

Part 4 – a very small number of names nominated by bishops for pastoral reasons, outside of disciplinary procedures, subject to satisfactory rights of representation by the clerics concerned.

Beyond these periods of time the cleric could request the Tribunal (or the archbishop in Part 4) to remove the record as allowed for in Chapter 7 (paragraph 23).

10

THE FINANCIAL IMPLICATIONS OF DISCIPLINE

Introduction

10.1   What will the cost of our proposals be to the Church and how will these costs compare with those that have been incurred by the system which is currently in operation? In this chapter we try to answer these questions.

10.2   One of the strongest criticisms of the present disciplinary system is its cost which is said to be unreasonably high. The costs incurred in the trials of the Reverend Thomas Tyler and the Dean of Lincoln are cited in support of this. We found ourselves in some sympathy with this viewpoint. However, we would wish to focus on some salient facts that must be borne in mind as we consider this controversial area.

(a)   A disciplinary procedure cannot be permitted to be governed by economic criteria. Clearly we desire cost effectiveness and value for money; but the requirements of a fair hearing for the accused, and adequate opportunity for the case in defence of the accusations to be heard, cannot be set aside or discounted purely to save money.

(b)   The existing Consistory Court procedures carry with them an inevitable level of expense. We are confident that our proposed Tribunal system will be significantly less costly. *But it will still involve expense.* The more strident criticisms of the current position almost imply a demand for a cost-free disciplinary procedure. This is totally unrealistic and must be clearly stated to be such.

(c)   For a clergy 'work force' in excess of 10,000, the Church of England is prepared to spend over £5 million per year in initial training before a person is ordained. Beyond ordination it spends very little, either in ongoing training and appraisal, or in discipline, by comparison with secular employment. The balance between initial training costs and ongoing disciplinary expenses is uneven. There is a case for suggesting, overall, that the Church spends surprisingly little on discipline.

(d)   For a cleric accused of an ecclesiastical offence, it is difficult to seek advice from the diocesan registrar, because the registrar is likely to be the bishop's legal adviser and also registrar of the Consistory Court that would hear a trial. So the cleric concerned is quite likely to turn to other legal professionals for help. Very often these will be lawyers with little or no competence in ecclesiastical law and procedures. This immediately implies additional potential cost, as they will need to research those aspects of law as well as providing their normal services to their clerical client.

10.3   We have not tried to devise a system 'on the cheap'. An effective disciplinary system will inevitably need to be properly resourced both in monetary and other terms; but we have been looking to produce a system which is fair both to the accused and to the wider Church. We do, however, believe that a system based on our proposals will provide better value for money. However, whilst we can make certain basic assumptions about the likely costs, what we cannot forecast is the extent to which a system based on our proposals would be used. As we have noted elsewhere in this Report, only three cases have been tried under the 1963 Measure, but we believe that this is partly because the Church's experience of that legislation has inhibited the bringing of cases. If, as we hope, a new system is one which is more flexible and with which the Church is comfortable, an increase in the number of cases is a likely consequence. Any costs offset in an individual case compared to a case under the 1963 Measure could be more than made up through an increase in the number of cases being heard.

10.4   During our deliberations, representations were made to us that members of the legal profession should give their services free in discipline cases on the analogy of surgeons doing this in the treatment of clergy at St Luke's Hospital for the Clergy. We are aware of some lawyers who have done this in the recent past but we were conscious that this could not be legislated for, and that, if this were to happen, it would have to be in the form of proposals from the profession itself. We understand that the Ecclesiastical Law Society now has a Working Party examining these issues. However, the difficulties – such as solicitors in partnerships needing to make their proper contribution to the profit costs of the firm – should not be underestimated.

Costs under the 1963 Measure

10.5   Costs to the Church fall under three broad headings: expenditure by way of Legal Aid granted to the accused under the Church of England (Legal Aid) Measure 1994 (and earlier enactments); the costs incurred by the bishop of the diocese; and the costs associated with court expenses.

(a)   The Legal Aid Fund is maintained by the Central Board of Finance on behalf of the General Synod. Under the Legal Aid Measure it is partly funded by way of contributions made to the General Synod Fund by the dioceses, and partly through contributions made by the Church Commissioners, each of whom may make such contributions to it as they shall determine. The custom has been that each body contributes half of the costs.

(b)   With regard to costs incurred by bishops, under section 58 of the 1963 Measure, the Commissioners have power to pay out of their general fund the whole or part of the costs and expenses incurred by a bishop or archbishop (not himself being the accused person) or someone nominated as promoter in connection with proceedings under the 1963 Measure. The Commissioners are given an absolute discretion but we understand that, in reality, they generally have little choice but to pay, although the section does entitle them to satisfy themselves that the amount involved is reasonable.

(c) Section 62 of the 1963 Measure requires the Central Board of Finance to pay the costs and expenses of all courts, commissions, committees and examiners constituted under the Measure in respect of offences, except in so far as some other person is liable to pay for them. As with the Legal Aid Fund, the 1963 Measure empowers the Church Commissioners to contribute out of their general fund such sums as they consider fit to relieve the Board of this liability, and the Commissioners customarily contribute half of such costs.

10.6 The actual costs of the three cases tried under the 1963 Measure under these three headings have been as follows (there were, of course, two trials and appeals in the Tyler case):

THE REVEREND MICHAEL BLAND (1969/70)

Legal Aid	£14,792
Bishop's costs	£5,423
Court costs	£1,514

THE REVEREND THOMAS TYLER (1991/2)

Legal Aid	£170,106
Bishop's costs	£108,801
Court costs	£37,686

THE DEAN OF LINCOLN (1995)

Legal Aid	£32,038
Bishop's costs	£50,107
Court costs	£17,680

10.7   These, however, are not the only costs that have been incurred under the Measure. Although only three cases have proceeded to a full trial in the Consistory Court there will be other cases which have not proceeded to that stage (for example where the censure by consent procedures in section 31 have been utilised), but where expenses will necessarily have been incurred. In the case of bishops' expenses, the annual cost to the Church Commissioners has varied between nil and nearly £9,000 over the last six years (this figure, of course, *excludes* the costs of those cases referred to above which went to trial).

10.8   As can be seen, no direct costs under the 1963 Measure fall upon the dioceses themselves (which is not the case in proceedings under the Incumbents (Vacation of Benefices) Measures), although undoubtedly there will be hidden costs involved.

Costs of our tribunal based system

10.9   As indicated above, the overall cost of a disciplinary system based on our proposals cannot be calculated because we cannot anticipate how frequently the system will be utilised. However, we believe that, in any particular case, the costs will be less. Taking the three categories of expense mentioned above, we would comment as follows.

(a)   In the figures for the three cases listed above, a significant proportion of the expense was, in each case, on legal aid. This is of course outside our terms of reference as such although nothing in our recommendations would inhibit the right of an accused cleric to be properly represented in disciplinary proceedings. In any event the Ecclesiastical Legal Aid system has recently been thoroughly reviewed by the Synod and there is now a new Measure and Rules which govern the administration of the Ecclesiastical Legal Aid system. The Synod must, therefore, be satisfied with the system as it is now operated.

(b)   Under our proposals those expenses which bishops incur will be dealt with differently. These will still be met by the centre but will be incurred in the prosecution of cases by the Church's central Legal Department. It will be for that department to decide, in the light of the volume of work being generated and the fact that advocacy work will be required, whether its existing legal staff are able to take on this work, whether an additional lawyer will be required, or whether outside firms should be instructed to undertake this work. The precise way in which this might work out will need to be discussed against the background of the process of implementing the recommendations of the Archbishops' Commission on the Organisation of the Church of England.

(c)   We believe that the costs identified above as 'Court costs' will be less because the tribunal based system which we recommend is considerably less elaborate than the procedures leading to a trial in the Consistory Court. Our proposals also allow a case to be heard in private and the use of existing church properties on reimbursement of fuel and running costs. This will mean that the expenses incurred in hiring appropriate venues, and the paraphernalia that goes with it, will be considerably less.

10.10   To complete the picture we must mention the costs of the support structures to our tribunal based disciplinary system. First will be the costs of the Clergy Discipline Commission (whose responsibilities are set out in Chapter 7, paragraph 16). We do not see these costs as being any more than those of other such bodies, for example the Legal Aid Commission. As far as the investigators are concerned (paragraph 7.20) we envisage that these will be remunerated on an expenses only basis. The President and registrar of the Clargy Discipline Tribunal will of course need to be remunerated, possibly by way of a retainer, but this will be offset by the fact that the individual diocesan registrars will no longer be registrars of the Consistory Courts in disciplinary matters, and therefore no longer remunerated for any work done in that capacity.

11

Summary of Recommendations

Our recommendations are summarised as follows. At the end of each recommendation is a reference to the chapter and paragraph number where these recommendations are set out.

General recommendations

11.1   The Church should 'go back to the drawing board' in revising its disciplinary structures (2.7 and 3.42). Only Part 1 of the 1963 Measure should be retained in its present form (5.2 & 3).

11.2   The rules of natural justice should be adhered to (3.30 and 39).

11.3   The bishop's role in clergy discipline should be reaffirmed. He must be involved early in the process and be given a sufficient degree of flexibility (4.6-8).

11.4   Any new system must give the bishop the assistance needed to help him reconcile his disciplinary and pastoral roles (4.6 and 7).

11.5   The Archbishops' Caution List should be reviewed. It should become the official depository of decisions made under due disciplinary process. The scope for including the names of clerics on the List who have not been involved in disciplinary procedures should be reduced (5.14-18; 7.23).

11.6   The law concerning clergy who do not hold a freehold office should be amended so that:

(a)   fixed term licences should not be revocable on notice;

(b)   where a cleric continues in office after the expiry of a fixed term, three months' notice of termination of the appointment should be necessary. If the cleric continues in office for more than twelve months the licence should become an indefinite one;

(c)   licences should generally be for a fixed term; but, where a licence is indefinite, it should not be revocable for disciplinary reasons;

(d)   the Church's disciplinary procedures should be followed for licensed clergy as they would be for freehold clergy (5.28).

11.7   The Measure to implement our proposals should require the formulation of guidance Codes of Practice covering all aspects of clergy discipline (3.40 and 41; 5.29 and 30; 8.17-19).

11.8   Disciplinary proceedings should, with certain exceptions, be held in private, but the decision should be pronounced in public (5.34).

11.9   No disciplinary procedures should be brought against a cleric for any political *opinions* which he holds, but the existing provision in relation to political *activity* should be abolished (5.36).

11.10   The Church should provide all ordinands with an explanation of its disciplinary processes (5.40 and 41).

11.11   Alongside a new disciplinary system, the General Synod should provide an appropriate grievance procedure (5.39).

The scope of discipline

11.12   The Church's disciplinary processes should apply to all in Holy Orders whether freehold or licensed, stipendiary or not, active or retired (6.1).

11.13   The following should be regarded as disciplinary offences for which proceedings under the disciplinary processes may be invoked:

(a)   wilful disobedience to or breach of the laws ecclesiastical (6.15);

(b)   neglect, culpable carelessness or gross inefficiency in the performance of the duties of office (6.16);

(c)   conduct inappropriate or unbecoming the office and work of a Clerk in Holy Orders (6.17 and 20);

(d) teaching, preaching, publishing or professing doctrine or belief incompatible with that of the Church of England as expressed within its formularies (6.18);

(e) conviction in a secular court of an offence for which a sentence of imprisonment can be imposed (6.19).

11.14 Where a cleric is involved in a divorce or a judicial separation a review of the circumstances should be made to establish whether there are grounds for invoking the disciplinary processes (6.22).

The core structures

11.15 All disciplinary complaints should be dealt with under a single procedure (7.3).

11.16 The forum for adjudicating all disciplinary complaints should be an independent national tribunal ('The Clergy Discipline Tribunal'), not the dioceses' Consistory Courts and the Court of Ecclesiastical Causes Reserved (7.5).

11.17 The Tribunal would be under the overall direction of a legally qualified President (7.8) and would be administered, on a day to day basis, by its registrar (7.9).

11.18 In any particular case the Tribunal should be chaired by a legally qualified Chairman appointed by the President from a specially established panel (7.10). The Chairman would sit with a clerical and a lay member, again drawn from panels, making a total of three (7.11).

11.19 The Chairman would rule on points of law but other decisions would be taken by a majority of the members. In ceremonial, ritual or doctrine cases, special assessors would be appointed (7.13).

11.20 The procedures of the Tribunal would be governed by Rules and the standard required to convict should continue to be proof beyond reasonable doubt (7.14).

11.21 A new body, the Clergy Discipline Commission, should be established. Its members would be members of General Synod and its functions would be: to maintain the lay and clergy panels from which members of a Tribunal would be drawn, and a panel of investigators; to advise bishops; and to act as a policy and resource body. It would report to Synod (7.15).

11.22 Prosecutions in disciplinary cases should be the responsibility of the Church's central Legal Services Department although others may be instructed by the Department to do some or all of the work (7.19).

11.23 The Clergy Discipline Commission should maintain a list of investigators whose role would be, under the auspices of the legal department, to investigate complaints and to collect evidence (7.20).

The core procedures

11.24 The procedure for the making of a complaint alleging an ecclesiastical offence should be uncomplicated. Anyone should be able to make a complaint (8.7).

11.25 Upon receiving a written complaint (not, at this stage, a 'formal complaint') the bishop would have a period of four weeks within which he, or more usually a person to whom he delegates the task, would make 'soundings' about the complaint (8.8).

11.26 After the initial period the bishop should make one of four decisions:

(a)   the complaint is dismissed as clearly vexatious;

(b)   the complaint has some substance but is of a minor nature. A procedure dealing with minor complaints is followed;

(c)   as (b) but, because the gravity of the complaint is difficult to define, the minor complaints procedure is followed unless the seriousness of the complaint becomes more obvious. The bishop may direct that the matter should be dealt with under the Incumbents (Vacation of Benefices) Measures procedures;

(d)   the complaint is of a more serious nature. The bishop invokes the disciplinary processes and the complainant is asked to complete an official complaint form (8.9 and 21).

11.27   If formal disciplinary processes are invoked, one of the following actions should be taken by the bishop:

(a)   after investigation he may decide to take no formal action (8.31);

(b)   he may refer the matter for conciliation (8.32);

(c)   he may impose a penalty if the cleric consents to it (8.35);

(d)   he may decide that the complaint should be investigated and prosecuted (8.39).

11.28   The bishop should have power to suspend a cleric at any stage. The cleric should be able to ask for a review of this suspension (8.42).

11.29   Where the person complained of is a bishop, the same procedures, with necessary modifications, should be followed (8.45).

11.30   The Incumbents (Vacation of Benefices) Measures 1977 and 1993 should be modified so that they extend to infirm cathedral clergy and archdeacons and ineffective clergy holding any office (8.46).

11.31   Appeals against a decision of a Tribunal may be made to the Arches or Chancery Courts. The Dean of the Arches/Auditor would hear the appeal sitting with two tribunal chairmen (8.47).

11.32   Appeals may be made as of right against the penalty imposed or, with leave, on a point of law or where it is alleged that the decision is unreasonable (8.48).

11.33   Resignations, in disciplinary circumstances, should not be accepted and acted upon without reflection and should not be allowed to circumvent its being recorded as a disciplinary matter (8.50).

Ecclesiastical disciplinary penalties

11.34   Where a cleric is found guilty the tribunal should be able to impose any of the following penalties (9.16):

- removal from office
- disqualification
- prohibition

- injunction
- conditional discharge
- deferred sentence
- rebuke
- absolute discharge

11.35   If the penalty is for an indefinite prohibition of the exercise of orders, the bishop may proceed to deposition from Holy Orders (9.16 (c)).

11.36   Where the penalty is disqualification or prohibition (and the bishop has not proceeded to deposition), the cleric may, after due time, apply to the Tribunal for the lifting of the penalty (9.16 (b) and (c)).

11.37   When the bishop gives censure by consent, the same penalties should be available to him, except that:

- in the case of prohibition he should refer it to the Tribunal for ratification;
- in the case of an injunction he should refer it to the Tribunal because disregard of the injunction would constitute contempt of court (9.18).

11.38   A cleric should be able to request the Tribunal to consider removing a record beyond a certain period of time (9.22).

THE WORKING PARTY

Membership

Chairman:	The Reverend Canon Alan Hawker (Chichester)
Members:	Mrs Janet Atkinson (Durham)
	The Bishop of Beverley (the Rt Rev John Gaisford)*
	Canon Joan Collinson*
	Mrs Margaret Laird (Third Church Estates Commissioner)
	The Archdeacon of Plymouth (the Ven. Robin Ellis)
	Mr David Wright (Oxford)
Corresponding member:	The Dean of the Arches (Sir John Owen)

(* The Bishop of Beverley and Canon Collinson were both members of General Synod at the time of their appointment. They ceased to be members of the General Synod in October 1995 and were then reappointed to the Working Party, as non-Synod members, for the duration of the Working Party's life.)

Assessors:	Mr Peter Beesley (Ecclesiastical Law Association)
	Mrs Lesley Farrall (Diocesan Secretaries Conference)
	Mr Nick Richens (Ecclesiastical Law Association)
Secretariat:	Mr Brian Hanson
	Mr Malcolm Taylor

Number of meetings

We met on fourteen occasions during the course of 1995 and 1996. All of these meetings were for the greater part of a day. All of the costs of our meetings, which mainly comprised expenses for travel and subsistence, were met from the General Synod's budget for its legislative programme.

We also had a joint meeting with the Clergy Conditions of Service Steering Group and, on a later occasion, two of our number joined a small group established to discuss clergy complaints and grievance procedures and related issues.

APPENDIX B

LIST OF SUBMISSIONS

At the outset of our work we invited submissions from members of the General Synod and, through the Church Press, the wider Church. We also specifically sought evidence from certain other Churches, bodies and individuals.

Submissions received

We examined existing (or, where appropriate, proposed) disciplinary systems in the following Churches and professions:

Church of Canada
Episcopal Church in the United States of America
Church in Wales
Scottish Episcopal Church
United Reformed Church
Assemblies of God

General Medical Council
The Law Society

We considered submissions from the following bodies and individuals:

The Legal Aid Commission
The Ecclesiastical Judges Association
The Secretary to the Advisory Board for Ministry
The Ecclesiastical Law Society
Broken Rites
The Church Commissioners
The Central Board of Finance
The Manufacturing, Science and Finance Union (Clergy Section)

Archdeacon of Blackburn
Archdeacon of Newark
Bishop Donald Arden
Bishop John Bickersteth
Bishop of Chichester

Bishop of Crediton
Captain David Brown
Chancellor Peter Farrant
Chancellor the Revd Rupert Bursell
Chancellor Quintin Edwards
Dr G. R. Evans
Dr Frank Robson (Oxford Diocesan Registrar)
Mr Alastair Black
Mr Richard Bloor
Mr David Cheetham (St Albans Diocesan Registrar)
Mr David Faull (London Diocesan Registrar)
Mr Raymond Hemingray (Peterborough Diocesan Registrar)
Mr Clifford Hodgetts (Chichester Diocesan Registrar)
Mr Tom Jordan (Hereford Diocesan Registrar)
Mr Lionel Lennox (York Diocesan Registrar)
Mr G. L. E. Locke
Mr Alan McAllester (Chester Diocesan Registrar)
Mr Brian McHenry
Mr David Phillips (Chelmsford Diocesan Secretary)
Mr J. S. Walker
Mr Derek Wellman (Lincoln Diocesan Registrar)
Mr Peter White (Winchester Diocesan Registrar)
The Revd Dr R. T. Beckwith
The Revd J. Cross
The Revd C. Fane
The Revd W. Y. Kingston
The Revd M. G. Smith
The Revd R. S. Stokes
The Diocese of Hereford
The Diocese of Lincoln
The Diocese of Worcester

We also considered a small number of confidential submissions principally concerning the Archbishops' Caution List.

We heard oral evidence from:

The Bishop of Norwich
Dr Frank Robson
The Dean of the Arches

APPENDIX C

Prepared by the Clergy Conditions
of Service Steering Group

OTHER CHANGES NEEDED
TO COMPLEMENT A NEW
DISCIPLINARY SYSTEM

Introduction

C.1   This Appendix looks at what arrangements might be needed to complement the formal disciplinary system proposed in the main text. It has been produced by the Clergy Conditions of Service Steering Group, after consultation with the Clergy Discipline Working Party, since the matters it covers fall outside the latter's terms of reference.

The consultation highlighted three areas that merited comment alongside the proposals on clergy discipline. These were:

(a)   providing a procedure for *minor complaints* that fall short of the need for discipline;

(b)   clarifying the boundaries of *ministerial review*, so that this is clearly demarcated from disciplinary procedures; and

(c)   suggesting a *grievance* procedure to allow clergy to express their concern when they feel poorly handled by senior clergy.

Wide ranging consultation will be necessary if these matters are deemed appropriate to progress. This Appendix is therefore offered as a basis for further discussion. The Steering Group's approach differs significantly from that of the Working Party, in that it sees introducing new complaints procedures as part of the wider programme of improving clergy conditions of service endorsed by the General Synod in November 1995. But it also views the recommendations covered in this Appendix as crucial complements to the new disciplinary procedures.

Procedures for resolving minor complaints about the clergy

DEFINING 'MINOR COMPLAINTS'

C.3 The Steering Group draws a distinction between: 'complaints', which fall short of being disciplinary matters; clergy 'grievances' relating to some aspect of their conditions of service or treatment; allegations of 'ecclesiastical offences', which it considers to be 'disciplinary matters'; and allegations of criminal activity. In some cases it might become evident that a complaint should be a disciplinary matter, but the Steering Group sets out below recommended procedures for dealing with a matter understood *at that time* to be a complaint. Such resolution procedures would be used for all manner of lesser allegations of the clergy 'falling short' or showing inefficiency, such as failing to take advertised services or simply being rude. (In fact in the case of many minor complaints an apology or an informal oral rebuke may be all that is required and the full complaints process would not need to come into play). How 'falling short' might be defined is examined below. The action taken to deal with complaints should not be recorded in the disciplinary record (Part 1 of the 'Caution List').

C.4 The concept of 'falling short' of the standards required is one familiar to those involved in personnel matters in the secular world. It is widely recognised, not least by industrial tribunals, that it is unreasonable in many contexts to expect a formal statement of required performance standards. However, there is other material which can give an indication of expected performance levels – e.g. a job description or a staff handbook. The Steering Group considers that such an approach is also appropriate for the clergy. It would be unrealistic to set performance levels in terms of number of services, length of sermons, etc.; but (as Chapter 3 of this Report illustrates) there is material, such as canon law regarding the duties of parochial clergy, case law, the Bishop's Regulations for Non-Stipendiary Ministry (ABM Policy Paper No. 5), the Ordinal and the 'Bishop's Handbooks' which exist in some dioceses, which is relevant to the idea of having a criterion of 'falling short'. The Steering Group considers that this type of approach would be appropriate for getting to grips with the complex concept of the Church's expectations of its clergy.

THE NEED FOR NEW COMPLAINTS RESOLUTION PROCEDURES

C.5   The Steering Group sees complaints resolution procedures as an essential complement to new disciplinary arrangements. Without them, many of the complaints which would be lodged would unnecessarily end up in the disciplinary processes, with a resultant waste of time and resources. Effective complaints resolution procedures would save the Church money, by providing an inexpensive vehicle for administering justice in respect of minor matters. The absence of satisfactory procedures for dealing with complaints was noted in submissions both to the Clergy Conditions of Service Steering Group's consultation exercise and to the Clergy Discipline Working Party. The Steering Group also sees formalising complaints resolution procedures as a significant step towards improving the conditions of service of the clergy. Such procedures could be helpful for a number of reasons:

- the impersonal nature of formal procedures helps people to see them as fair;

- a framework would exist within which individuals could reasonably make criticisms, and which would prevent those in authority avoiding issues which were difficult;

- the clergy, laity and bishops would know where they stood;

- by formalising procedures that previously existed in some places only in custom and practice, any ambiguities and inconsistencies within them would be clarified;

- and by providing pre-established avenues for responses to various contingencies the responses would be less random and so fairer.

PRINCIPLES OF A COMPLAINTS RESOLUTION PROCEDURE

C.6 Complaints resolution procedures must be grounded in the principles of natural justice set out in Chapter 3. But they should be proportionate to the matters with which they are to deal: that is, they should not be elaborate and all matters should be dealt with at the lowest possible level. The procedures (particularly with regard to outcome) should also encapsulate the biblical principles of reconciliation and healing. Without compromising fairness, procedures should be flexible, simple and accessible to all. Bona fide complainants should not run the risk of themselves becoming the subject of sanction.

C.7 All clergy sometimes 'fall short', but complaints resolution procedures must recognise that it is rare that their wrongdoing is sufficiently grave that formal procedures need to be considered. Regrettably, while such wrongdoing may be rare, complaints are not. As was noted in Chapter 3, the public profile of the clergy makes them especially vulnerable to attack. Particular care must be taken to protect the clergy from unwarranted allegations. The procedures must deal robustly with malicious and mischievous complaints, yet must be such as to reveal the truth. They should protect the innocent, whilst ensuring that those who have erred can be held to account.

STRUCTURE OF A COMPLAINTS RESOLUTION PROCEDURE

C.8 The Steering Group recommends, therefore, that complaints resolution procedures should be set up on a diocesan basis, with as few people as possible dealing with complaints and with the personal involvement of the diocesan bishop kept to the minimum. The procedures established should be publicised.

C.9 A suggested model for such procedures is outlined below.

Informal Stage

(a) Someone with a complaint about a cleric should raise it at an early stage in the appropriate context – e.g. on a one-to-one basis with the other person concerned. The complaints resolution procedures recommended here should not be considered as the first or only option for seeking resolution of minor complaints about the clergy. The procedure should only be used when the complaint is about a potentially significant matter.

Formal Stage

(b)   If it is not possible for the matter to be settled informally, or attempts to resolve the difficulty through informal means have failed, a specific complaint based on hard evidence should be lodged with the diocesan bishop (unless the complaint is about the diocesan bishop, in which case see below).

(c)   The bishop should form a preliminary view as to whether there is a potentially significant problem. If the complaint is trivial, capable of immediate resolution or stems from malice, the bishop should take such action as he feels to be appropriate. If the matter seems to be potentially disciplinary or criminal in nature, the relevant procedures for dealing with cases of this nature (set out elsewhere in this report) should be followed.

(d)   Assuming that the complaint is potentially significant and not capable of immediate resolution, the bishop should take care not to become involved at this stage with its handling, so that he can ultimately be brought in at the appeal stage if necessary. He should nominate a suitably trained cleric to look into the matter and rule as appropriate. (The Steering Group considers that a cleric is the right choice for dealing with *minor* complaints, since a cleric is most likely to be able to deal with minor problems expeditiously, 'in-house', without undue 'fuss'). This person, who might be a rural dean or an archdeacon, should have the powers to recommend a solution and the necessary changes if the complaint were to be upheld, and would need to hold a post at least at the 'level' above the cleric complained about (e.g. archdeacon in the case of a complaint about an incumbent).

(e)   The person nominated by the bishop should look carefully into the matter and seek resolution through conciliation wherever possible. The emphasis should be upon using common sense and aiming to heal.

(f)   The procedures for dealing with the complaint should be relatively informal but encapsulate the spirit of natural justice.

(g)   If consensus is not achieved, the person nominated by the bishop should decide what action should be taken. This decision should be made known to the complainant, the cleric complained about and anyone responsible for taking the action recommended. A dissatisfied complainant, or the cleric complained about, would be able to appeal to the diocesan bishop.

Appeal

(h)   The diocesan bishop should consider and decide about any complaint referred to him on appeal.

Procedures in the event of a complaint about a diocesan bishop

The procedures set out above assume that the complaint was about a cleric other than the diocesan bishop. If the complaint is about the diocesan bishop, it should be referred to the archbishop of the province in the first instance. If the archbishop's provisional view is that there is a potentially significant complaint not capable of immediate resolution, he should appoint a diocesan bishop to look into the matter. Any appeal would then be to the archbishop.

CREATIVE APPROACHES TO DEALING WITH PROBLEMS WHICH COMPLAINTS MAY BRING TO LIGHT

C.10   One of the characteristics of the procedures for dealing with complaints should be a creative and constructive approach to dealing with difficulties that are identified. Often a complaint will serve to highlight a need for training, so the links with Continuing Ministerial Education should be strong. Other complaints may point to the need for advice, e.g. on how better to handle pastoral situations. Potential sources of such advice should be identified in advance. The formal and informal support structures for the cleric and his family must also be reliable. The emphasis should be on the pastoral dimension and avoiding recurrence of the difficulty, rather than taking sanctions.

C. 11 There will be rare and extreme cases where complaints about a cleric bring to light reasons which point to the need to explore whether full-time stipendiary ministry should cease. Certain clergy may, for example, feel that their vocation is leading them to serve as a lay person; others may be suffering from ill-health or infirmity, such that further full-time ministry is no longer practicable. The Church should have a range of established procedures for dealing with such situations, and must take seriously its moral responsibility for the clergy. It cannot be over-emphasised that a cleric has frequently given up a well-paid job and a house upon entering the stipendiary ministry; and that this commitment, which is often sacrificial in nature, also frequently involves clergy families. The Steering Group therefore welcomes the ABM's Policy Paper Number 4, 'Moving Out of Full-Time Ministry', which offers a creative approach to clergy in the sort of situations described. In particular, the Steering Group welcomes the recommendation that any severance payment (apart from any housing provision) should have regard to that which would be statutorily required if the clergy were employees and the legislation for redundancy were to have applied. The Group also welcomes the emphasis in the paper on pastoral care and the need to seek constructive solutions which are acceptable to the Church as a whole and to the individual cleric.

RECORDING OF ACTION ON COMPLAINTS

C.12 The pattern of complaints should be monitored by a person nominated by the diocesan bishop. Confidential written records of the actions taken to deal with minor complaints notified to the bishop should be made. As was noted in the context of discipline (Chapter 3, paragraph 44 and Chapter 7, paragraph 22), a more rigorous and systematic recording of telephone conversations and interviews would be necessary than is typically current practice. Strict confidentiality would need to be respected concerning the records kept. The outcome of a complaint should be recorded on the bishop's staff file for the person involved, but not on the Caution List. The action involved should range up to a letter of advice, but not beyond. The recording of such action could, it should be noted, ultimately have disciplinary implications. If a pattern of complaints emerged, e.g. a vicar repeatedly failing to take the required services, a disciplinary process might ensue. In such circumstances the record of complaints would constitute part of the evidence.

COMPARISON WITH SECULAR COMPLAINTS RESOLUTION PROCEDURES

C.13 In drawing up these recommendations the Steering Group was conscious of the parallels with the secular world, but also of the differences from it. It drew on material from ACAS and employment law, but adapted these to the particular structures and needs of the Church. It did so not out of a bureaucratic desire for formality or because of managerialism, but in response to calls from the clergy for improvement of their conditions of service. The Group believes that this is one area in which the secular employment legislation sets out a standard of good practice to which the Church ought to aspire by introducing procedures of its own suitable to its particular needs.

RESOURCE IMPLICATIONS OF THE PROPOSED NEW COMPLAINTS RESOLUTION PROCEDURES

C.14 The Steering Group's suggestions would inevitably have resource implications, but it believes that the cost would not be great and would be small in comparison with the benefits. For the Church to set up new complaints resolution procedures there would need to be a programme of publicity about the new procedures and suitable in-service training for those clerics to be involved in handling complaints. There would also be costs involved in the process of consultation over drawing up detailed procedures. But the Group believes that this is a price well worth paying for two reasons: first, because effective complaints resolution procedures would in the long run save money which would otherwise be spent on disciplinary actions; secondly, because the Church would be seen to have fair and open procedures.

Ministerial review

OVERVIEW

C.15 Arrangements for ministerial review were considered by the General Synod in the context of the November 1995 debate on 'Improving Clergy Conditions of Service'. One of the report's recommendations was that 'ministerial review [was] a key aspect of clergy conditions of service and that as a major priority dioceses should undertake the development of effective systems of review in accordance with the Advisory Board of Ministry's Paper Number 6 ("Ministerial Review: Its Purpose and Practice")'. Effective systems of ministerial review are needed for all the clergy, stipendiary and non-stipendiary. However, such systems require significant resources, including adequate time set aside, training for those involved, preparation, and a monitoring system. The Clergy Conditions of Service Steering Group hopes that Bishops will give a lead to ensure that effective systems are in place. The Steering Group hopes too that more resources will be made available at the national level to monitor ministerial review systems and to encourage good practice nationally. This would require additional resources for this function in the Advisory Board of Ministry (where recent cuts have reduced the staff resource available for this). In the longer term, it may well be that if the Turnbull Report's vision of a 'Resources for Ministry' department becomes a reality this would be an opportunity to re-direct resources available for this purpose.

C.16 The purpose and nature of ministerial review schemes must be clear. The Steering Group believes that a ministerial review system should not be expected, for example, to pick up evidence of disciplinary problems or those few clergy who are significantly 'falling short' in some way. Some of these problems may happen to reveal themselves, but there can be no guarantee of this and ministerial review should not be designed specifically to reveal such matters. Set out below are the reasons for drawing a line between ministerial review on the one hand and disciplinary problems (minor and major) on the other.

C.17 The Advisory Board of Ministry (ABM) noted in its Ministry Paper Number 6 that in the 42 mainland dioceses there were 50 schemes of ministerial review, with 15 different underlying purposes. The ABM found this an unsatisfactory situation, and it encouraged greater consistency. The ABM also recommended that ministerial review systems should be primarily developmental, that is about enhancing the effectiveness of the clergy's ministry, and not about sanctions for under-performance. Developmental systems involve clergy being self-motivated and willing to reflect on their own experience and potential training needs in a non-threatening environment. Such a review, which ought to happen at least once a year, does not need regularly to involve a bishop or archdeacon. It may be done with peers or with lay people, provided that they are specially trained to undertake such work. Input should be encouraged from all those associated with the person's ministry - including churchwardens in particular. The Steering Group believes such systems can work well provided that arrangements are in place to ensure that training needs are identified and communicated to the diocese's Continuing Ministerial Education Officer. They also overcome the practical difficulty stemming from the bishop's being 'Father in God' to so many clergy; for it is unrealistic to set up a system in which the bishop would have personally to conduct an annual ministerial review for all the clergy in his diocese. There is also some evidence that developmental, peer-based systems are the most effective in encouraging and motivating clergy. For example, a number of schemes directly involving bishops have simply collapsed when a diocesan bishop has left and where the scheme has primarily been 'owned' by him and not by the clergy as a whole.

C.18 The Group believes, therefore, that it is best to focus ministerial review systems on that which they do best - the development and affirmation of the exercise of a person's ministry. The situation nationally is much better than it was, say, ten years ago, but dioceses need to learn from one another's experiences of ministerial review and to adapt their systems accordingly. By so doing the Church can encourage and support its clergy and enhance their effectiveness in mission and evangelism.

THE SCOPE FOR 'BISHOP'S REVIEW'

C.19 The demands on bishops' diaries and the 'hierarchical' relationship between the bishop and his clergy are not, the Group considers, conducive to successful developmental ministerial review. Bishops and archdeacons need to meet the clergy regularly for a number of reasons, including:

- to pastor the cleric (including those not in the parochial ministry) and the cleric's family;

- to get to know the cleric's parishes better (churchwardens may have a useful input here);

- to look at the cleric's ministry in relation to the ministry of the diocese;

- to consider whether a move might be in the cleric's interest or that of the whole Church;

- and to develop a shared view of the priorities for ministry in the area.

Such contact must have a developmental aspect, but it should, the Group considers, be a complement to peer-based review, rather than an alternative to it.

RECOMMENDATIONS ABOUT MINISTERIAL REVIEW

C.20 The Clergy Conditions of Service Steering Group is therefore working with the ABM on producing a proposal to encourage the Church to move in such a direction: to harmonise existing ministerial review schemes and to aim for dioceses operating their variants of two main models: a peer review scheme concerned with development, learning and affirmation of a person's exercise of their present ministry; and a system of 'Bishop's review' aimed at establishing healthy pastoral relationships and looking at the person's ministry in the context of the diocese as a whole. *Neither of these exercises would be part of disciplinary arrangements, since such concerns are of a quite different order.*

Clergy grievance resolution procedures

DEFINING 'GRIEVANCES'

C.21 For the purposes of this Appendix, 'grievance' is taken to refer to a complaint brought by a cleric about some aspect of conditions of service or treatment. Thus a 'grievance' differs from a 'complaint' in a number of ways:

- in its **source,** in that it comes from a cleric;

- in its **link with disciplinary systems,** in that this connection is weak – a grievance is less likely than a complaint to bring to light a disciplinary matter;

- and in its **nature,** in that there may not be a specific cleric being complained about.

THE CALLS FOR NEW GRIEVANCE RESOLUTION PROCEDURES

C.22 The national consultative exercise about clergy conditions of service conducted in 1994-5 revealed that clergy and others felt that grievance resolution procedures needed to be improved; several of the representations to the Clergy Discipline Working Party made the same point. The Steering Group questions whether the present arrangements in dioceses work effectively to ensure fair play in the working relationship between the clergy and the Church as a whole. The Steering Group considers that inadequate grievance resolution procedures can have a corrosive effect on clergy morale. Good channels of communication for clergy grievances would allow most problems to be tackled before they fester. Such mechanisms would also be needed to call to account, not aggressively but quietly, senior clergy if they had 'fallen short' in the treatment of fellow members of the clergy. Introducing new procedures for dealing with grievances would be a significant improvement of clergy conditions of service.

PRINCIPLES OF GRIEVANCE RESOLUTION PROCEDURES

C.23 The Group considers that the principles for dealing with clergy grievances should mirror those for dealing with complaints. That is, they should:

- be grounded in the principles of natural justice;

- demonstrate a commitment to healing and reconciliation;

- deal with matters at the lowest possible level;

- filter out malicious and trivial grievances;

- allow a cleric with a genuine grievance to pursue it without fear of becoming the subject of sanction;

- and be used only for the purposes for which they were designed.

THE STRUCTURE OF A POSSIBLE MODEL FOR CLERGY GRIEVANCE RESOLUTION PROCEDURES

C.24 A recommended model is set out below for diocesan based clergy grievance resolution procedures which are similar to those for dealing with complaints. Again, the personal involvement of the diocesan bishop is kept to the minimum and the model is based on a common-sense, relatively informal approach.

Informal stage

(a)   A cleric with a grievance should raise it at an early stage in the appropriate context – e.g. in a 'Bishop's review', through talking to a peer or on a one-to-one basis with the other person concerned. The clergy grievance structures recommended here should not be considered as the first or only option for seeking resolution of clergy dissatisfaction. They should not be used as a channel for communicating general discontent or, except as a last resort, for concerns for which other resolution systems exist (e.g. complaints about clergy housing).

Formal stage

(b)   If it is not possible for the matter to be settled informally, or resolution of the difficulty through informal means has failed, a specific grievance based on hard evidence should be lodged with the diocesan bishop (unless the grievance is about the diocesan bishop, in which case see below).

(c)   The bishop should form a preliminary view as to whether there is a potentially significant problem. If the grievance is capable of immediate resolution, or stems from malice, the bishop should take such action as he feels to be appropriate. If the matter seems to be potentially disciplinary or criminal in nature, the relevant procedures for dealing with cases of this nature should be employed.

(d)   Assuming that the grievance is potentially significant and not capable of immediate resolution, the bishop should take care not to become involved at this stage with the handling of the clergy grievance, so that he can ultimately be brought in at the appeal stage if necessary. He should nominate a suitably trained cleric, with powers to recommend action and the necessary changes if the grievance were to be upheld, to look into the matter and rule as appropriate. This person might be a rural dean or an archdeacon, and would need to hold a post at least at the 'level' above any person complained about.

(e)   The cleric nominated by the bishop should look carefully into the matter and seek resolution through conciliation wherever possible. The emphasis should be upon using common sense and aiming to heal.

(f)   The procedures for dealing with the complaint should be relatively informal but encapsulate the spirit of natural justice.

(g)   If consensus is not achieved and other action is necessary, the person nominated by the bishop should so rule. This decision should be made known to the person with the grievance, any person complained about and anyone responsible for taking the action recommended. A cleric with a grievance or any cleric complained about who is dissatisfied with the decision, would be able to appeal to the diocesan bishop.

Appeal

(h)   The diocesan bishop should consider and rule on any clergy grievance referred to him on appeal.

Procedures in the event of a clergy grievance about a diocesan bishop

The procedures set out above assume that the clergy grievance was about a cleric other than the diocesan bishop. If the clergy grievance is about the diocesan bishop, it should be referred to the archbishop of the province in the first instance. If the archbishop's provisional view is that there is a potentially significant clergy grievance, he should appoint a diocesan bishop to look into the matter. Any appeal would then be to the archbishop.

RECORDING OF ACTION ON GRIEVANCES

C.25   As with complaints, the pattern of grievances should be monitored by diocesan bishops. Written records of the actions taken to deal with grievances notified to the bishop should be made and strict confidentiality for records should be respected throughout. The expected outcome of grievance procedures should be mediation rather than sanction. On the rare occasions that action was ultimately taken against a cleric, this should be recorded on the bishop's staff file for the person involved, but not on the Caution List. The action involved should range up to a letter of advice, but not beyond. Only if a pattern emerged of repeated misdeeds would grievance records be likely to have disciplinary implications.

RESOURCE IMPLICATIONS OF THE PROPOSED NEW GRIEVANCE RESOLUTION PROCEDURES

C.26 The Steering Group considers that the resource implications of its proposals – relating to in-service training, publicity about the new arrangements, and other such arrangements similar to those needed to implement the proposals about complaints – would not be great. The benefit to the Church would be a significant improvement in the conditions of service of its clergy and a system which was much fairer than present arrangements.

Safeguards for clergy without the freehold

C.27 The Group welcomes the way in which the Clergy Discipline Working Party has highlighted one aspect of the lack of security for clergy without the freehold: the bishop's power to revoke a licence for disciplinary reasons without due process. The Steering Group has in fact encouraged the ABM to bring forward proposals for improving more generally the security of clergy without the freehold. The ABM's Ministry Development and Deployment Committee is looking at just this issue, with a view to making recommendations for change.

Process for introducing new minor complaints and grievance resolution procedures

C.28 The Steering Group believes that it has identified a significant shortcoming of the present conditions of service of the clergy: namely that new procedures are needed in respect of complaints about the clergy and grievances which they hold. A suggested outline of procedures for dealing with these situations is set out above. The Group is, however, conscious that before the ideas are developed further there should be a process of thorough consultation with all the interested parties before specific decisions are made. The General Synod is therefore invited to endorse the general principle of the introduction of new minor complaints and grievance resolution procedures, with a view to these proposals subsequently being sharpened up in consultation with the clergy themselves (including the House of Bishops), Diocesan Offices, the Advisory Board of Ministry and others. The eventual systems might be incorporated in a Code of Practice to stand alongside those for disciplinary procedures.

Conclusions

C.29 The Clergy Conditions of Service Steering Group considers that the matters covered in this Appendix are an important complement to the proposed changes to the statutory discipline system. The Group also considers that they are essential elements of a strategy to improve the conditions of service of the clergy and to improve the Church's 'personnel practices'.

C.30 In drawing up these recommendations, the Group was acutely conscious that in secular organisations the area of complaints and grievance resolution procedures was usually handled by a specialist personnel resource. This partly reflects the complexity of the matters involved and of the way in which the law is involved; but it also reflects the fact that these matters are directly concerned with the welfare of the individual and the health of the organisation. The Church has few people specifically employed as personnel (as opposed to pastoral) specialists. The Church rightly places a high priority on pastoral relationships; it places a lower priority at the moment on the related but distinct area of human resource or personnel management. The Church's most precious resource is its people, and among those are the clergy and those the Church employs. Safeguarding their conditions of service, developing the individual and stewarding the Church's human resources must be crucial to the furthering of mission. The Steering Group is convinced, therefore, that as a long term aim the improving of clergy conditions of service should be complemented by an enhancement of the Church's personnel and human resource management capability, for example through improved training and through giving greater priority to personnel matters.

Recommendations

C.31 The Clergy Conditions of Service Steering Group recommends the following:

(a) a consultation exercise to be carried out with a view to dioceses adopting new minor complaints and clergy grievance procedures based on a national Code of Practice;

(b) continued efforts to develop in dioceses systems of ministerial review which would not form part of disciplinary arrangements; and

(c) continued efforts to enhance the Church's personnel and human resource management capability through improved training etc.